W9-DGH-227

SIX LECTURES ON ARCHITECTURE

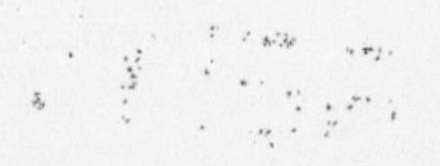

SIX LECTURES ON ARCHITECTURE

BY

RALPH ADAMS CRAM
THOMAS HASTINGS
CLAUDE BRAGDON

Essay Index Reprint Series

THE SCAMMON LECTURES FOR 1915
PUBLISHED FOR THE ART INSTITUTE
OF CHICAGO BY THE UNIVERSITY OF
CHICAGO PRESS, CHICAGO, ILLINOIS

BOOKS FOR LIBRARIES PRESS
FREEPORT, NEW YORK

First Published 1917
Reprinted 1968

Reprinted from a copy in the collections of
The New York Public Library
Astor, Lenox and Tilden Foundations

LIBRARY OF CONGRESS CATALOG CARD NUMBER:
68-57314

NOTE

THE lectures presented in this volume comprise the eleventh series delivered at the Art Institute of Chicago on the Scammon foundation. The Scammon Lectureship is established on an ample basis by the bequest of Mrs. Maria Sheldon Scammon, who died in 1901. The will prescribes that these lectures shall be upon the history, theory, and practice of the fine arts (meaning thereby the graphic and plastic arts), by persons of distinction or authority on the subject on which they lecture, such lectures to be primarily for the benefit of the students of the Art Institute, and secondarily for members and other persons. The lectures are known as "The Scammon Lectures."

TABLE OF CONTENTS

LIST OF ILLUSTRATIONS

[The illustrations face the pages designated unless otherwise indicated.]

LECTURE I

LECTURE II

LECTURE III

LECTURE IV

LIST OF ILLUSTRATIONS—*Continued*

LECTURE V

LECTURE VI

THE PROMISE AND THE FULFILMENT OF GOTHIC ARCHITECTURE

BY

RALPH ADAMS CRAM

I

THE BEGINNINGS OF GOTHIC ART

All great architecture is organic; every building that has endured, or will endure, as a monument of good art is, in a very real sense, a living organism. Like the horse, the tiger, or the eagle, all its parts are perfectly adapted to their function, admirably co-ordinated, determined by exact considerations of the adaptation of means to end, and expressed in forms and lines that are in themselves beautiful. Like man, it also is possessed of spirit, and the combination of these two elements gives it an actual life and almost places it in the category of the creatures that exist by the will, and at the hand, of God.

The variations in style between one century and another are as human variations in race and speech, and as those wide intervals that separate one epoch of high civilization from another of a correspondingly low type, or from those intermediate stages which form the major part of history. Like the life it so closely resembles and so exactly represents, architecture is a thing of infinite but rhythmical vicissitudes, with brief periods of supreme achievement interspersed with long intervals of slow rise and swift decline, and again, like life, it shows no progressive growth, no tendency toward earthly perfection. If there are moments when the art crests in such splendid accomplishment as occurred in Greece, in Byzantium, in the Middle Ages, it cannot be said that as a whole the later manifestations reached higher levels than the earlier, their individual excellence being only in certain categories.

In every case, however, there is a close relationship between this art (and its allied arts) and the civilization that brought it into being. There is no great art with an immediately antecedent condition of barbarism; there is no degraded art in close succession from a high civilization. Art and life do not synchronize; they form a sequence, and as art itself comes at and after the cresting of a wave of human development, we often find a strange contemporaneousness of noble art and a civilization that already has begun to decay.

To understand a style, therefore, it is necessary to do more than scrutinize its material elements, determining by scientific methods its line of stylistic descent and the peculiarities of its organic mechanism. This is, it must be admitted, the usual course, and it lands both historian and student in such a dilemma as that which confronts those who, confining their scrutiny to the material elements alone, find the Gothic of France the most logical and perfectly worked-out manifestation of a style that was almost Europe-wide, and therefore, since the other national modes fall short of this, deny to these even the once derided, now universally revered, style of "Gothic."

This process is less architectural history and criticism than it is architectural biology and pathology. In architecture, as in all arts, in all existence, it is the spirit that giveth life; and it is not the forms, it is the spirit behind and within Greek, Byzantine, Gothic, and Chinese Buddhist architecture that makes each live, as do not the other epochs of its varied and illuminating career.

Fully to understand the great significance of that era of architectural growth which, beginning roughly with the year 1000, goes on with ever-increasing vigor until it culminates about three centuries later, we should have to study not alone the rise of Romanesque, its transition into the first Gothic, its astounding climax in the first quarter of the thirteenth century, and its slow and splendid decay through another two hundred years; we should also have to merge ourselves in the intricate history of this great period of five centuries, in its political and economic development, its philosophical adventures, its crusades and guilds and communes, above all in those religious experiences and determinations that are its greatest exemplification as they are its underlying cause.

Manifestly this is impossible within the scope of two lectures. It is the labor of years (if it is not the illumination of a moment) and not now for us. All we can do is to note the most salient points and block out the main lines of what I hope for many may be subsequently a study as revealing as it is absorbing.

I need not remind you of the original significance of the word "Gothic"—how it was given in scorn by the self-sufficient amateurs of the Renaissance to the art they had inherited but could neither appreciate nor rival. To them the word and the work meant anything barbarous and illiterate, and illuminating as this is on the point of their own intelligence, it is, I think, hardly so discreditable as is that effort, of which I have already spoken, on the part of modern commentators to reduce one of the most inspired and inspiring arts to the terms of a few structural formulae. Gothic architecture and Gothic art were an impulse and a tendency: as the Greeks took the simplest conceivable architectural norm and developed it to final perfection, so the mediaeval builders took the most complicated problem and tried to develop it to that point of perfection which they saw in some beatific vision, and which was actually beyond the power of man to attain.

Of course they failed; but they left, not a perfected thing subject neither to change nor to improvement, but a stimulating force ever inciting men to take up the work they left unfinished, and high-heartedly to strive once more to achieve the unattainable.

To this extent it was a greater art than had been known before; for its aim was higher, its goal more clearly revealed, and this goal was that which lies at the very root of art itself, viz., the symbolical expression of otherwise inexpressible ideas, i.e., those which by their very nature are so high that they transcend all ordinary and direct modes of human expression. Consciously or unconsciously, mediaeval art was at bottom sacramental, and this explains, in a way, its immortality, its constantly recurring appeal, as it explains the same immortality and appeal by sacramental religion and sacramental philosophy —as of St. Bernard and St. Thomas Aquinas and Hugh of St. Victor—for it is only such art, such philosophy, such religion, that will permanently endure, since these alone are in eternal conformity with life, which also is essentially and unchangeably sacramental.

Between mediaeval civilization and mediaeval art the connection was so close as to amount to practical identity. Rheims, Freiburg, Canterbury, are simply the Middle Ages made visible and translated into the terms of an enduring and dynamic influence. All the joy of life, the vivid vitality, the humor, romance, and mysticism, the simplicity and naïveté of that opulent age find outlet through the wrought stone and wood, glass, and metal that assembled under eager hands and at the impulse of ardent brains to create that plexus of all the arts, a mediaeval cathedral. We may read history without limit and delve in original records for years without acquiring as much sense of the real mediaevalism as we could obtain through a day in Bourges or York or Strasburg—if only there we could find what once was: all the arts assembled together to make a Mass as it was before the shrines and altars and windows were broken, and the bizarre music and tawdry ceremonial of the nineteenth century took the place of the massive Gregorians and the solemn ritual of the fourteenth century. Even now, however, in such a church as Chartres

SANT' AMBROGIO—INTERIOR

or Seville it is possible to re-create the dead past, as is impossible in schoolroom or study or lecture-hall.

Gothic art is a great unit, and into this enter certain traditional, ethnic, and religious elements that determine, not only its spirit, but its form as well. Under the first heading we have all the classical heritage from Rome and the East through the Latin South of France and the pseudo-Byzantine Carolingians; under the second, the dominating northern blood, which, whether Frank, Norman, or Burgundian, wholly succeeded and dominated the decadent blood of the South; under the third, that all-embracing Catholicism which was the moving and regenerating force, directing, controlling, inspiring, through monastic establishments, military orders, and the crusades.

The Romanesque of the eleventh and twelfth centuries in all Europe, the Gothic of the thirteenth, fourteenth, and fifteenth centuries in Flanders, France, Spain, and England, were the direct expression of the greatest and most beneficent religious reformation ever recorded in Christendom, carrying in its train a civil reformation that redeemed western civilization from the Dark Ages and built up for the first time a great and measurably consistent Christian society. It shows it; for of all art it is at once the most competent and the most inspired, mingled equally of active reason, good sense, brilliant thinking, and a spiritual emphasis, a final idealism that we may search long in world-annals to equal.

Beginning at the hands of monks of many orders, this art infused the whole Church, being taken up at last by the bishops and focused in the vast and innumerable cathedrals, and so extended through the laity, high and low, until it became an intimate and indispensable attribute of life itself.

The material and structural development of Gothic architecture was a result neither of sudden revelation nor of headlong evolution; it was a phenomenon of slow and logical growth. In plan, structure, and organism, it reaches back through Norman, Romanesque, Lombard, Byzantine, and Syrian trails to Rome itself. Even in the basilicas of the Eternal City we find the nave and aisles separated by columns and arches, the colonnaded triforium and clerestory, the transept, choir, and apse. Transferred to the shores of the Bosporus, the Roman mode of building is divided into two followings—the basilican and the domical. Here they are separated, the Eski Djouma and St. Demetrius in Salonica being very noble examples of the first;

Aya Sophia in the same city, SS. Sergius and Bacchus, the churches of the Pantokrator and the Chora, and of course Aya Sophia itself, in Constantinople, immortal examples of the second. Both are strictly Roman in origin; but as under Constantine the basilican type was vastly enriched and developed over its Roman prototype, so under Justinian the domical and cellular motive was elaborated into the almost unimaginable splendor of that most glorious church, where, after five centuries of alien occupation, we are now permitted to believe that we ourselves may see the Christian Sacrifice offered once more in petition and in expiation.

In Syria and Byzantium, Roman architecture first became structurally and artistically consistent, and the work of Justinian, through his Greek architects and under a majestic religious faith blended with the Christianized splendor of the East, must be considered as one of the great styles in history. Perfect as it was in all its internal organism and decoration, it never worked out a corresponding exterior, although, when both basilican and domical types were imported into Italy and Greece under the Exarchs, in certain places, particularly in the latter, this last development began, as in the exquisite little monasteries of Styris and Daphne.

It was too late, however; the stimulus of a vital civilization had passed, and the evolution was left for other hands and other races. This came in part with the introduction of the strong northern blood of the Lombards. The old basilican mode had been carried on in Rome on Christian lines after the Edict of Milan in 313, but the Lombards after 568 introduced a totally new spirit, and in Toscanella, and later in Pisa, Verona, Lucca, Milan, we see the striking results of a radically new departure marked by an impulse as northern as all that had gone before had been southern.

Venice was always a splendid anachronism, a Byzantine colony in the midst of aliens, and St. Mark's is not in the line of architectural descent, which for the future was to be under the direction of the supreme North.

There was, however, one element of great mystery and equal uncertainty, the influence of the Comacini. There are those who attribute to them all that afterward was evolved under the Carolings, the Normans, and the Franks; others who look on them as half mythical and wholly ineffective. For my own part, I incline, for once, toward a middle ground, believing in their undoubted existence and their persistent influence, but finding in the new and vital power of northern blood, fixed by monastic fervor for righteousness, not only the unique bent toward new and splendid things, but also the *élan* that alone could revitalize a tradition already moribund.

These Comacini were the colonies or guilds of free builders (some call them free masons and the progenitors of the modern secret societies of the same name) who fled from Rome in the midst of its downfall and sought refuge on an island in Lake Como, in a region still under the evanescent protection of the empire of New Rome, or Byzantium. They are held to have brought with them in their exile, not only the traditions of Roman building, but dim memories and symbolisms from the East, even from Jerusalem itself. Here, in this island refuge, were preserved through the Dark Ages the sole surviving tradition of the old building of the days of classical culture, and when at last Charlemagne desired to restore the art of architecture again, it is from this island that he drew his builders, who thereafter spread slowly over Europe, founding new lodges and transmitting to their successors the methods and secrets and traditions of the immortal past.

Much of the evidence to support this theory is circumstantial, but it must be admitted that it is cumulative and generally convincing, and those who are interested in an obscure and tempting quest may follow it readily in Leader Scott's *Cathedral Builders*, which, while not always reliable as to dates and attributions, is full of an immense amount of incontestible testimony.

That the early "Lombard" work of the eighth century in Italy, as at Toscanella, is novel and vividly original as well as competent and beautiful, is undeniable, and the peculiar qualities there shown reveal themselves century after century in Normandy, Burgundy, and the Rhine country, as well as in Lombardy itself, until in the twelfth century they come full-flower in Padua, Verona, Pavia, Milan, Lucca, and Pisa. In Italy it is a distinguished and an exquisite style, vital and intelligent, quick with invention, and with a certain wild charm that well covers its—sometimes refreshing—naïveté and even barbarism. In the North it shows itself in many ways, though here rather as a bending, not a controlling, influence. We find it at Cluny, at Jumièges, at Caen, and it is impossible now to say how much of this persistent and wide-spread quality may be due to the successors of the old Roman guilds, how much to the latent force in the Lombardic race. Some line of succession was operative, influencing many peoples in many lands and spreading far and wide, not methods

DURHAM CATHEDRAL—WEST FRONT

of building alone, not types of ornament such as the interlacing strands and the wild things from the forests, but an elaborate and mystical system of symbolism as well, so fully worked out that the monk Durandus in the eleventh century had it all at his finger ends.

Between the two types we are considering, the question was live loads versus dead loads. The basilica was inactive; its small nave arches had little thrust and its apse semi-dome also; the great triumphal arch to the choir was the only thing that was seriously active. The domical structure, even when its domes and vaults were of concrete, was always pushing in every direction and putting a premium on that ingenuity that was always busy devising balancing thrusts. In spite of its simplicity and inexpensiveness, the basilica yielded to the dome, partly for material considerations of permanence and fire protection, partly because the northern mind was not content with easy tasks. By 900 A.D., in Sant' Eustorgio in Milan, transverse arches were being thrown across the aisles from each pier, thus involving the first rudimentary buttresses. In 985, as at the Church of Santi Felice e Fortunato in Vicenza, these transverse arches were thrown across the nave itself, as long before in Syria, usually on the alternating system. Then from the domical buildings of Syria, Byzantium, and Ravenna came the masonry vaulting of the smaller areas, and at last the masonry construction of the high vault.

Before this last innovation, which brought the whole system of Gothic construction and organism in its train, the ribbed vault had to be devised. When this happened no one knows, but it was probably a northern invention and meant the ultimate transformation of the simple Roman organism into the most nervous and highly articulated creation of the hand of man. The aisle rib vaults at Montefiascone *may* be original; if so, they date from 1032. The high vault of Sant' Ambrogio is also doubtful and may be of the year 1060. The present weight of evidence points to Normandy, or even Durham in England, where the ribbed vault is of the year 1093, but for my own part I believe it is Lombard; for it is exactly in line with other undoubted inventions of the same ingenious race.

Whatever its source, this ribbed and domed vault was the greatest discovery of man in architecture, after the arch and the dome, and its suppleness, adaptability, and perversity in the matter of thrusts were stimulating to a degree.

The development of the compound pier and archivolt and of the alternating system followed hand in hand with the evolution of the ribbed and domed vault. The oblong vaulting spaces for the nave, in place of square areas, were worked out in Normandy through the abbeys of Caen, by means of sexpartite stages, and at last the flying buttress, which has grown from the arched abutments of Sant' Ambrogio, through the half-barrel vaults of the Abbaye aux Hommes, to the true flying buttress of the Abbaye des Dames, which was still modestly concealed below the roof. At Noyon, about 1260, it emerged into the light of day, and at the same time the pointed arch, which is first recorded in France in the Abbey of Cluny at the end of the eleventh century, achieved complete acceptance, partly because of its adaptability, chiefly because of its beauty, and not at all because it aided in the vaulting of oblong compartments—as is so often claimed—simply because it never was so used, the device of stilting having already solved that problem and made possible those subtle waved surfaces that were and are the joy of the architect.

In the processes thus far narrated we have acquired most of the elements in the Gothic system: compound shaft and arch, ribbed, domed, and stilted vaults (quadripartite, sexpartite, and oblong), buttresses, flying buttresses, pointed arches, while the vertical system of arcade, triforium, and clerestory, and the great west towers are fully established through such monuments as Jumièges, the abbeys of Caen, St. Germer de Fly, and St. Denis. With the last building comes the perfected chevet, that incomparable masterpiece of mediaeval genius, with its polygonal apse, doubled aisles, and ring of chapels. At first it would seem that this was a special creation of Gothic intelligence, if not of divine revelation, but stupendous as it is, it was a development of successive stages from a very old and equally simple norm. What has happened was this, and I think it very interesting.

The Syrian builders of the dioceses of Damascus and Antioch had taken the primitive Roman basilica—secular and pagan—and added to the east end that semicircular apse which first appears here in one or two heathen temples of the early second century. They thus obtained the standard type of the Christian basilica which has persisted even to this day, whatever may have been its racial impulse or its stylistic expression. Then they cut this apsed basilica in two and took the simple semicircular apse with its semi-dome to see what they could make of it. They made much. First they completed it into a circle; then they developed the little curved niches of some of the early apses into true, but subordinate, apses, applied directly to the perimeter of the circle; they next raised the wall to provide a clerestory of windows and encircled the whole at the ground level with a polygonal aisle. The memory of this early form in Syria is still preserved in the much later San Vitale at Ravenna. The result was a great organism, though not perfectly articulated. In such a church as that at Bosrah, however, this defect was remedied; for here the aisle encircles the central dome, and the apses are pushed to the outer wall. The articulation is now complete, and aesthetically the result affords the most wonderful play of light and shade imaginable. On the basis of this unique development—which surely worked itself out in the great days of the Church in Antioch and was utterly forgotten under the desolation that followed the Moslem invasions, even until the last century—were reared all the wonderful structures of Byzantium, of Charlemagne, and of Southern France, as for example, Aya Sophia, Aix-la-Chapelle, and Toulouse. By the introduction of a square area between two apses, and with its dome supported on pendentives—a device already used in Syria—and with its aisle curtailed and raised into two stories, we have the first; with an increase of height and the introduction of a triforium level, the second; while in the apse of the third we find the most extraordinary change of all—nothing less than the cutting of the circle in halves again, the full evolution having been accomplished, and the application of this half to its original position at the end of the old basilica, now equally transformed. Behold, then, with the other newly devised elements I have already named, and with its articulation raised to the point of finality, Bourges, Chartres, Rheims, Westminster—the finished and ineffable product, the definitive Gothic church.

Such is the structural evolution from 200 A.D. until 1100 A.D., one of the most remarkable exemplifications of the power of human intellect when it is infused by a vital religious faith and—for the last six of these nine centuries at least—by clean new blood and an almost abnormal vitality. In this process certain buildings stand as milestones, though we must always remember that, so far as dates are concerned, this credit may be partially undeserved, since it is possible, if not probable, that the truly era-making works—those, that is, in which some master-builder struck out first of all men some revolutionary and prolific device—have been utterly destroyed or buried under the desert sand of Moslem devastation or the heaped débris of revolution. On

ABBAYE AUX DAMES, CAEN—INTERIOR

the basis of what remains, however, these buildings are: the church at Bosrah, Charlemagne's church at Aix-la-Chapelle, Sant' Ambrogio, Jumièges, the two abbeys of Caen, St. Germer de Fly, and St. Denis. In the first two of these we find the promise and potency of the chevet; in the third, the germs that were to develop into at least three of the essential elements of Gothic; in the fourth, the main qualities of Gothic mass and organism; in the two Caen abbeys, the norm of all French cathedrals on the one hand, of all English abbeys and cathedrals on the other; in St. Germer, the actual chevet itself, as the North translated and glorified the dim prophecies of the East; and in St. Denis, the final gathering up of everything in preparation for the great flowering that was to come in less than fifty years. It was a masterly sequence, and it postulates a great civilization behind; for after all, thus far we have considered only the structural evolution. The qualities which give all this art, whether Byzantine, Romanesque, or Gothic, its supreme character are those subtle qualities of beauty, inspiration, and evocative power which are the vivifying spirit of great art and follow only from a potent civilization.

Now while there was no violent revolution, no artificial swerving of the line of development, such as occurred, for example, in the case of the Renaissance, there was a great transformation in the spirit that was working in the world and dominating it. If we are to gain any idea of what this was and why it was so potent, you must bear with me while I revert to a little ancient, and very ancient, history.

By the year 500 Rome had fallen, and classical civilization had become a name. Over the disappearing frontiers of empire poured the hordes of northern barbarians, and only the successor of St. Peter was left in a desolated city to bear witness against anarchy, heresy, and chaos. And yet, in the crash of toppling empires, in the North the king of the Franks was baptized, and in Rome itself Gregory the Great mounted the chair of Peter. From him went out the streams of energy that were to redeem and transform the northern hordes, through the agency of those monks who had accepted the Holy Rule of St. Benedict, who himself was the center and the energizing power of the new era that was to last for a thousand years.

Neither Rome nor its successor, Catholic civilization, was built in a day, and it took five full centuries to bring the work of St. Benedict to final fruition. There was a short-lived and partial success under Charlemagne, but ruin followed after, and it was not until 927 that St. Odo reformed the sterile Benedictinism of the Dark Ages and, through the order of Cluny, made it operative again as its great founder would have had it. Almost at the same moment Otto the Great restored civil order under a regenerated Holy Roman Empire, St. Bruno began the building of Germanic civilization, and Hugh Capet with Bishop Gerbert set out on their task of re-creating civilization in France. By the year 1000 the Normans had become fixed in Northern France, Christianized and ready for action; the curtain rose, and the splendid drama of mediaevalism began to unfold itself.

The first act is the era of a new Benedictinism and what we call Romanesque and Norman architecture. To this mode the Benedictine was always devoted, and he made it a thing of power and nobility and—in the end—inordinate richness. He began where Byzantium and Charlemagne left off; he re-created architecture on Christian lines, but he could not continue to the end, for the reason that monasticism, while indestructible in essence, is human in its agencies, therefore fallible, and doomed after each century to sink to a point where a reformation is imperative.

As the Cluniac wave so spent itself, it slipped slowly back into a very human corruption, and its art took on a splendor and a magnificence that defeated its own ends. Then came the inevitable reform in the shape of the great Cistercian revolt against luxury of life and laxity of morals and an unwholesome sumptuousness in art. The Cluniac and the Norman created Romanesque, the Cistercian and Frank created Gothic, and Gothic in its beginnings was a puritanical revolt against a too splendid art.

It was well that this should be so, for at once men's minds were turned from ornament to form, structure—in a word, to organism, which *is* architecture. The round arched Benedictine style was becoming a thing too costly to be endured; too costly in its enormous masses of masonry, too costly in its florid and superabundant decoration. At first St. Bernard would have not even a carved moulding, no stained glass, no costly furnishings, no sumptuous ceremonial, while the ingenuity of his master-workmen was exerted toward finding a system whereby, through a balancing of thrusts, the sheer bulk of building material in any structure could be reduced one-half.

They found it, and Gothic architecture was the result; but in the process—not of structural evolution, but of that social evolution which lay behind—they found and they created much else. Justly estimated, the eleventh is one of the most wonderful centuries in history; for then began, and with astonishing vigor, all those great movements that were to find their climax in what has been well called the "thirteenth, greatest of centuries." The monks of Cluny were spreading enlightenment and order from a thousand centers all over Europe. When Gerbert became pope as Sylvester II, the degradation of the Papacy came to an end, and such great pontiffs as Leo IX and Gregory VII assumed sovereign direction of Christian civilization. Heathenism and Mohammedanism were beaten back, the Slav and Germanic tribes (all but the Prussians) were Christianized, and into Britain, Italy, Sicily, the Levant, poured the Normans, bringing with them order and the Catholic faith. Schools were built on monastic foundations in every land, the merchant guilds came into being, art was reborn, and at last the flame of universal fervor culminated in the First Crusade.

As all architecture, and particularly Gothic architecture, is pre-eminently organic, so was the civilization that brought it into being and used it as its chosen mode of visible expression. The three centuries from 1000 A.D. to 1300 A.D.

were probably the most wholesomely organized and the most sanely balanced and the most physically and spiritually stimulating that Christian Europe has known—at least so far as France, England, and Germany (again omitting Prussia and Brandenburg, which were not even Christianized) are concerned. No one would deny the existence of violence, ignorance, corruption; but these things have always been and, if we are to judge from the present condition of the world, always will be. The point is that they were then less dominating, less mordant in their influence, than before or since, while they were largely neutralized, or at least mitigated, by other elements of supreme virtue and nobility that had issue in a society, a civil government, an art, a philosophy, and a religion that combined to produce a condition of life which has in history few rivals in the creation of fine human character.

It would be impossible to do more at this time than to indicate lines of possible study, as, for example, the origin and development under monastic influence of innumerable schools all over Europe, particularly schools of philosophy, medicine, and general culture; the growth of a specifically Catholic philosophy, on an essentially Greek foundation, but wholly Christian in its essence and destined to a final flowering in such

ELY CATHEDRAL—WEST FRONT

immortal figures as Duns Scotus, Hugh of St. Victor, and St. Thomas Aquinas; the appearance of the great merchant guilds, with the trade guilds to follow, and the organization of those landmarks in civil liberty and order, the village and city communes; the founding of those potent agencies of civilization, the military orders of knighthood and chivalry; the outburst of a creative and stimulating art that showed itself in music in the enrichment of the early plain-song, in the trouvères and troubadours; in poetry, in the *chansons de gestes*, and the Arthurian legends; in architecture in Pisa, Venice, San Miniato al Monte, Worms, Speyer, and Maintz, Poitiers, Le Puy, Angoulême, Arles, Toulouse, Vézelay, Clermont, Caen, St. Georges de Boscherville, Jumièges, Mt. St. Michel, in Canterbury, Winchester, Ely, Glastonbury, Durham; in the stained glass of Le Mans, Poitiers, Canterbury, and Chartres; in the metal work of Hildesheim, the sculpture of Autun, Moissac, and Chartres.

Finally, one might suggest study of some few of the great and splendid characters of the eleventh and twelfth centuries and of the causes that led to such an unheard-of galaxy of honorable names: St. Odo, St. Bruno, Otto the Great, Hugh Capet, Sylvester II, Hildebrand (Pope

Gregory VII), Chrétien de Troyes, Innocent III, St. Bernard, St. Anselm, St. Norbert, St. Thomas à Becket, Peter the Venerable, Suger, Abelard, Hugo of St. Victor, William of Champeaux, Lothair II, Richard Cœur de Lion, Henry II, Philip Augustus, Fulk of Anjou, Roger of Sicily, Matilda of Tuscany, Eleanor of Guienne, Blanche of Castile.

The great names coruscate like divine fireworks, and they were not isolated personalities in a wilderness of mediocrity or barbarism. The qualities they possessed in such supreme degree were merely intensifications of the general life in which they were merged. Racial and national self-consciousness, individual confidence and self-respect, industrial emancipation and development, all had become operative and dynamic influences, and the result was a sane, consistent, and character-building civilization that seemed to leave nothing for the thirteenth century. There was enough, however, as I shall try to show in my second lecture, when I propose to consider the development and full flowering of Gothic art, and though only superficially, some portion of the workings of the extraordinary *élan vital* that lay behind.

In the meantime, it is well to realize the amazing nature of the work accomplished between

St. Benedict and the First Crusade. It divides itself naturally into three parts, which may be called conservation, recovery, and expansion. For the first the monks of St. Benedict were responsible—and for much else besides. They, in their hidden monasteries that suddenly sprang up throughout all the West, collected and treasured the records of Latin culture, both sacred and profane, furnished refuges for men and women from the perennial blasts of destruction, and cherished, however dimly, the flame of righteousness and order, the tradition of such forgotten things as right and wrong. To them also belongs much of the credit of the second period of recovery, when, under the House of the Carolings, the world took breath again and set itself to build a new earth. Not much was accomplished perhaps—the day between the dawning of Charles Martel and the death of Louis the Pious was too short—but out of the dusty and mouldering monasteries came what had been saved from the wreck of worlds, and for a few years Charlemagne's court did indeed do much toward collating the treasure-trove and giving it, if not a new life, at least the potentiality for this when the time should be ripe.

With the eleventh century this time came; the unspeakable horrors of the second Dark Ages—

the ninth and tenth centuries—had reached a point when no further fall was possible. Feudalism—which had saved some semblance of order in the first Dark Ages—had become a combination of brutal slavery and insane anarchy. Kingship had ceased to be operative, culture was unknown, misery universal, the Papacy a stench and a blasphemy, and even the Benedictines themselves had sunk into a degeneracy from which there seemed no escape.

And yet there was an escape, as always when the world seems at the moment of extinction: the year 1000 marked, not the end of the world, but the end of an era; the new forces were working hiddenly, and when St. Odo founded the order of Cluny they came to the surface. At once this astonishing power became the great motive force in all Europe, reforming monasticism, purging the Papacy, wrenching the fangs of feudalism and secular control from the throat of the Church, restoring education, art, and culture, while indirectly assisting in the emancipation of the laborers and merchants and making possible the guilds and the city communes.

Individual self-respect, the sense of solidarity, and the national spirit grew apace, but perhaps the most potent development—potent in its guaranty of great centuries to follow—was the

VEZELAY CATHEDRAL—WEST DOORS

opening out of religion and its wide adaptation to the needs and the instincts of men. During the patristic period, whether in the East or the West, the constructive work in the developing and fixing of dogma had been largely intellectual. It was concerned primarily with destroying innumerable and poisonous heresies, with the fixing deeply of everlasting foundations. The passionate human element of St. Augustine was exceptional, but the time had now come for carrying still farther and developing more richly the tendencies he represented, so making Catholic Christianity forever a thing that met every demand and hunger of the human soul.

In the time of Charlemagne, Radbertus had put into definite form the full doctrine of transubstantiation, with all it meant of poignant appeal and the sense of divine immanence. Attempts to establish a strictly (as it was to be in later years) Calvinistic doctrine of foreordination and predestination were ruthlessly crushed; the tender and merciful aspects of Christianity were emphasized (though the methods were not always of that ilk); and sacramentalism, with its many modes of approach to God, its simple and obvious duties and benefits, interpenetrated the whole fabric of the ecclesiastical organism as well as that of secular society.

Finally, the place of the angels and saints, and particularly that of the Blessed Virgin, in the divine cosmogony, as conscious and affectionate friends, companions, and intercessors, was recognized and accepted as never before, with the result that by the beginning of the eleventh century religion had become, if not the most important thing in life, at least the most pervasive and appealing, influencing all secular and personal affairs and giving a unity and consistency to human effort and human existence such as had never been known before in history in any similar degree.

It was the *élan vital* of the Middle Ages, and its amazing workings were to have issue in that unique and consistent civilization, from the year 1100 to the year 1300, which, through its immortal artistic expression, I shall consider, though superficially, in my second lecture.

II

THE CULMINATION OF GOTHIC ARCHITECTURE

To some of those who are most deeply affected by the art of mediaevalism comes at times a questioning and a doubt. In the prose and metrical romances they find subtle delicacy, strong and sincere feeling, exquisite finish of workmanship; in the great Latin hymns, deep and poignant emotion coupled with a marvelous technical mastery; in the music of the Gregorian mode, an art of a perfection as unique as it is compelling; in Catholic philosophy, profound thought that is both analytical and constructive to an amazing degree; and in theology, a quite unparalleled mingling of keen recognition of human needs, of massive and logical constructiveness, of spiritual vision that transcends thought and lays hold of ultimate things. In the plastic arts they discover, as never before, sculpture that in beauty and in mastery of line and form matches only the best of Hellas, architecture that expresses itself as the most perfect organism veiled in the most delicately beautiful forms that history records, together with arts altogether new, as those of glass and tapestry and enamel, with, in every category, a handicraft that records no equal antecedents for eighteen hundred years.

By every law of analogy, every precedent of history, these conditions, if they are not fictions of autosuggestion, should argue the existence of a civilization and a culture of corresponding nobility and, necessarily, not only equal to that which produced the great art of classical times, but superior in all essential respects to that which followed it, since this, confessedly, had issue in a theology of doubtful value, a philosophy of—even now—contested authority and diminishing credit, and a complete downfall of all the arts save poetry and music and, in a few instances, the drama.

And against this they must set an almost universal, and a solemnly authoritative, assertion that behind this brilliant manifestation of culture and of character lay social chaos, political incapacity, universal warfare, cruelty, injustice, oppression, superstition, bigotry, Cimmerian ignorance, and all those elements of barbarism that go to the making of what we commonly know as the Dark Ages. The antithesis is striking, the paradox baffles the understanding, and as a result, it is to be feared, some are brought to the sorry pass of holding that after all there need be no vital connection between culture and civilization, and that art of any and every kind, lofty philosophy, and a loftier religion, need not be held to express anything of nobility or achievement in a nation or among a people, but may manifest themselves through savagery as they may disappear in an epoch of the highest development.

Such a lamentable deduction is quite unnecessary; for the paralyzing antithesis is only apparent. It has neither reality nor even plausibility, and is due partly to the misleading and wrong-headed nature of written histories, partly to a commonly inadequate and equally wrong-headed system of education, partly to a mental confusion and the loss of any adequate standard of comparative values that are the result of the two first-named agencies. Temperamentally incapable of estimating history except in terms of military operations, dynastic vicissitudes, or concrete material achievements, the popular historians, confused in the midst of the apparently aimless and resultless events and courses of the Middle Ages in these categories of unimportant activity, fall back on the conclusion that these are the full revelation of the time, that there was nothing in it anyway; and they write the history of the thirteenth century in the terms of Hohenstaufen and Capet and Plantaganet, of battles and councils and treaties and "pragmatic sanctions," of militant heresies and obscurantist scholasticism, of names and dates and titles. Where there are few indeed who write living history as Henry Adams writes it, or Henry Osborne Taylor, or Cardinal Gasquet, or John Richard Greene, or Lord Bryce, there are scores of the "baser sort," who mask their lack of vision and of comprehension by an erudition that almost persuades and by a heaping of the Pelion of genealogical records on the Ossa of military adventure that stuns if it does not enlighten.

If you would know the Middle Ages and why they brought into being the thing that was themselves—their culture—you must needs abandon the accepted historical method and consider, not the things that make facile textbooks, but those that make life and character and personality; for these were the essence of the Middle Ages, and they lie outside court and camp and council.

There is no little significance in the widespread and penetrating change now affecting the attitude of men toward the comparative position of

CHARTRES CATHEDRAL—INTERIOR

the arts of the Middle Ages, and toward its positive quality as well. There is still greater significance in the new estimate of the cultural background of this art. Before the events of the last five months of the year 1914 opened our eyes to the shallow and meaningless nature of our own civilization—until then so highly spoken of, if one remembers correctly—there were many who had gone back from mediaeval art to its social antecedents and accompaniments, who had rediscovered, and in some degree re-estimated, its philosophy and its religion, and who, rejecting the statistical history and the superficial diagnosis of current and popular chronicles, had found in the years between 1050 and 1300 a wonderland and a revelation. It is not to be forgotten that while the dominant tendencies in society were working themselves out, with neither let nor hindrance, to that logical culmination that revealed itself in the first week of that memorable August of the year of grace 1914, there was developing simultaneously a tendency as different as day from night, and with equal swiftness and even more startling vigor. Scientific efficiency, which—united to religious infidelity and state-worship—has been given the name of *Kultur*, was paralleled by a very opposite thing, which has always been known as culture, and this latter, made up of religion, philosophy, and art, was in its most essential elements based on the earlier culture, not of Hellenism, not of Roman imperialism, not of the Renaissance, not of the evolutionary philosophy and scientific efficiency of the nineteenth century, but on those very centuries from St. Bernard to St. Bonaventure, from Chrétien de Troyes to Dante, from Hildebrand to St. Louis, from Noyon to Beauvais, that had been forgotten for four hundred years and maligned by every historian during that same space of time.

Such a return, such a reaction, if you like, was inevitable. In my former lecture I tried to show something of the wonder of those crescent years from the close of the Dark Ages in 950 to the culmination of Catholic civilization three centuries later—those years that saw a new art, born from the ruins of a shattered past, work slowly through Norman and Romanesque and Burgundian modes toward the full flowering of perfected Gothic art. It is now for us to consider in a paragraph what justly requires many volumes—the continuation of this great era of growth and its intrinsic qualities that were the basis of the most comprehensive and inspiring art the world has known.

CULMINATION OF GOTHIC ART

The Middle Ages form a period of notably high culture but of comparatively undeveloped civilization. That this distinction is possible is proved by many eras of history, and it must be recognized if we are correctly to understand and estimate this particular period. Culture is made up of three elements—philosophy, religion, and art; civilization is measured by the degree to which a people has diverged from barbarism in motives, manners, and customs. Greece was a center of supreme culture, but her civilization was of no high order; Rome was superbly civilized, but in philosophy, religion, and art she fell immeasurably below the Greece she had destroyed. During the Middle Ages there was little ground gained in the recovery of the civilization that had disappeard, together with culture itself, during the Dark Ages. Manners at first were rude and direct, civil government rudimentary, industry carried on by very primitive methods, material efficiency almost unknown, and yet philosophy rose to transcendent heights, religion, both in theology and in action, was vital, commanding, loftily beautiful, and of a nature that endures forever, while art, in whatever category, rose out of the nothingness of the tenth to the dizzy heights of the thirteenth century, where it forms a goal of emulation thus far unattainable by succeeding generations. Civilization is an excellent means to an end, if that end be character or culture, but if it is unfruitful of either, or if it produces only the Dead Sea fruit of *Kultur*, it is no more than the tree that bringeth forth evil fruit, and it is cut down and cast into the fire. Culture, on the other hand, does not necessarily follow from civilization, nor does it always have issue in civilization or in that human character which is the object of life itself. Sometimes it casts its glamor over very evil conditions indeed, as in Greece and Byzantium, just as civilization blinds us to equally evil conditions in the later Renaissance, and in the nineteenth and twentieth centuries, when true culture is at a lower ebb than at any time for six hundred years. But the mediaeval period was not of this nature, and then, whatever we may say of efficient civilization, the culture of philosophy, religion, and art did produce character of the highest, while in itself it finds few rivals in the preceding centuries or in those that have followed.

From the twelfth century the thirteenth took over all the great creative theology of St. Anselm and St. Bernard and continued it to its logical conclusion through the Fourth Lateran Council. The pure piety and spiritual ardor of the great

BOURGES CATHEDRAL—NAVE

founder-monks of the preceding centuries blossomed into a world-wide monasticism that was in general the most stimulating and beneficent influence of the epoch, and closed at last in the perfect charity of St. Francis and the passionate ardor of St. Dominic. Catholic philosophy achieved its highest point in Albertus Magnus, Duns Scotus, Roger Bacon, St. Bonaventure, Raymond Lully, Alexander Hales, Hugh of St. Victor, and St. Thomas Aquinas. Now the Arthurian and Nibelungen epics take on their final form, the minnesingers and meistersingers follow the trouvères and troubadours, while Latin hymnology creates a new and glorious category of art, and Dante closes the line as the great synthesis, the culmination of all. Music perfected its Gregorian mode and began its development of harmony that was later to culminate in the eighteenth century after the death of the other arts; painting came into being through Duccio, Cimabue, and Giotto; sculpture in France, and later in Italy and England, recovered the spirit and the mastery of Greece; stained glass revealed itself in the amazing glories of Chartres, Bourges, Angers, as art of the greatest, while all the minor crafts of metal and wood and textiles followed suit, and toward an unexampled end.

Of the architecture of this amazing time I shall speak immediately, since this is the long-deferred object of this lecture; but first let me name one or two out of the galaxy that prove beyond cavil that here indeed culture, without the highest efficiency of civilization, was not inconsistent with the production of noble character. Note only such names as Innocent III, Gregory IX, Boniface VIII; Henry III and Edward I; Frederick Barbarossa, Rudolph of Hapsburgh, Ferdinand III, Alfonso the Wise, St. Louis of France, Stephen Langton, Robert Grosseteste, Blanche of Castile, St. Clare, St. Elizabeth of Hungary. Everywhere, on civil and ecclesiastical thrones, in cloister and on crusade, in the fast-multiplying universities—themselves the creation of mediaevalism—we find the most notable personalities, of a nature that establishes an undying hope for humanity and a guaranty of its powers of recuperation and lofty achievement.

The development of Catholic faith and practice along those personal and appealing lines, to which I have already referred, was the mainspring of the new vitality, and this development showed itself chiefly through an increasing richness and intimacy in the sacramental system and in the cult of our Lady and the saints. The crusades, which synchronize with the whole epoch of mediaevalism, the military orders of knighthood, and the splendid pageant of chivalry, all acted as connecting links between religion and secular life, knitting them for a few brief centuries into an organic whole. Everywhere, in all lands, on the hills, in the sheltered valleys, beside the unpolluted streams, were the monasteries, each with its free school and sometimes with its circulating library, the guiding spirit of youth, the inspirer of manhood, the refuge for old age. Universities with throngs of students rivaling the most numerous of those today—Prague, Paris, Padua, Montpellier, Orleans, Valencia, Valladolid, Oxford—grew to a position of power we can now hardly appreciate. In almost every great city was a free hospital with isolation wards for lepers and others afflicted with contagious diseases.

So far as the development of civil liberty, the formulating of law, and the organization of constitutional government are concerned, it is possible to say that more was accomplished in the Middle Ages than during any other equal period in human history. The Provisions of Oxford, Magna Carta, Bracton's *De Legibus*, the Codes of Frederic II, the Institutes of St. Louis, the Golden Bull of Andrew II of Hungary, the codices of canon law of Gregory IX and Boniface VIII, are the foundation stones of civil liberty and the basis of modern law.

Conditions of this kind are the forcing-house of art; it follows instinctively, without the intervention of schools or lectureships or wealthy amateurs. And it is a united art, expressing itself, not along one line alone, but in myriad ways. Architecture in the thirteenth century is no greater than sculpture, or poetry, or music, or glass; it is the vehicle of all, the plexus where all unite with one impulse and one end. It is a unity as perfect as that of Hellas, but it is different in its genesis and its operation; for it is a popular art, not the art of an elect caste; it is the work of free men, not of servile agents under a few of high attainments and high authority; and finally it is the expression of a personal and passionate religion that was life itself to every artist and every craftsman, every noble and every peasant, whose possession it was in fullest measure and without distinction of class or estate. It can truthfully be said that the word "Gothic" as applied to the plastic arts of mediaevalism is synonymous with the word "Catholic."

Not that the plastic arts then, or at any time, are alone entitled to be called art. The thing itself is greater than these and includes more, particularly poetry in every form, with music,

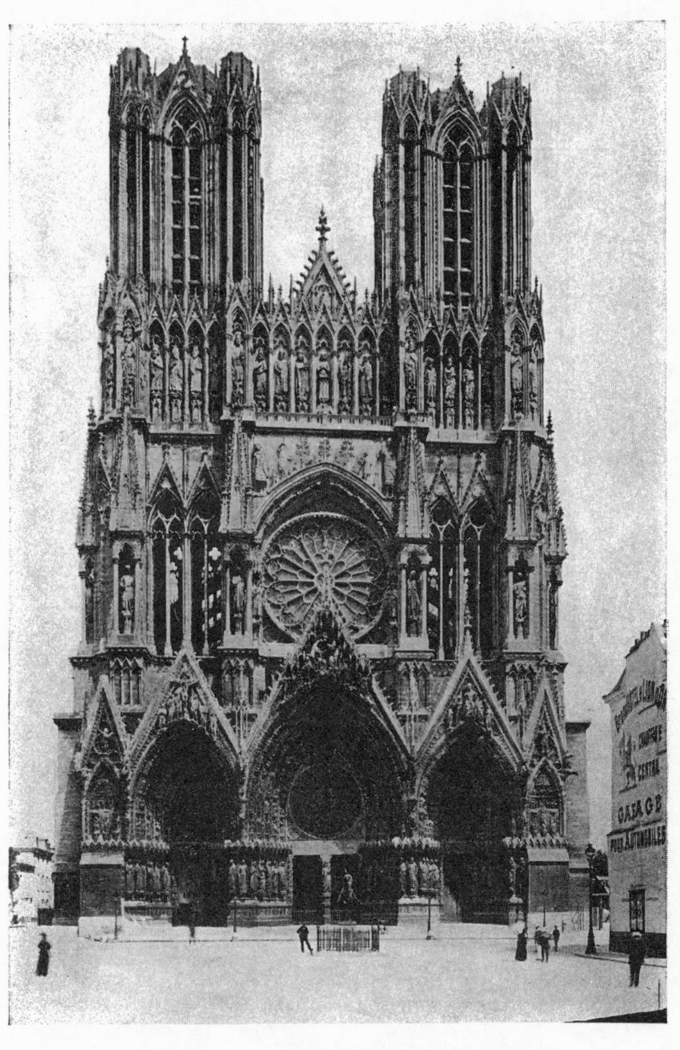

RHEIMS CATHEDRAL—WEST FRONT

drama, and ceremonial. The modern fashion of confining the "fine arts" to painting, sculpture, and architecture is evidence in itself how far we have fallen from the cultural ideal of the Middle Ages.

Now, architecture, as I said in my first lecture, is primarily organism; it is also synthesis, that is, it cannot exist without many of the other arts, and when—as in the case of a Gothic cathedral in operation—it combines with itself every other mode of art, then it becomes the greatest art-manifestation possible to fallen man. Chartres or Rheims or Westminster in the fourteenth century during a pontifical mass was undoubtedly the greatest and most comprehensive work of art the mind can conceive or the intelligence bring into being.

This organic quality on which I have laid so much stress, not only because of its essential importance, but also because it is the very quality most lacking today, was determined and assured in the twelfth century. The thirteenth was devoted to perfecting this to the highest possible point and to infusing the result with the spiritual elements of beauty and of emotional stimulus. In this the artists of the time were following a natural parallelism with such other commanding artists as Homer, Plato, Shakespeare, Michelangelo, all of whom found their enduring glory, less through original discovery and creation, than through their power of gathering up all the work of their forbears and breathing into it the breath of life.

This great work of organic development may be seen to perfection in the Cathedral of Our Lady of Paris, and it is progressive from east to west. The choir was begun in 1163, the west front completed in 1235, and in these seventy years all the promise of Jumièges was fulfilled in more than abundant measure. From east to west there is a steady growth in certainty of touch, in structural articulation and integrity, and in the development of the sense of pure beauty. The plan is of the simplest—only a parallelogram with one semicircular termination, divided into five aisles, the middle one being twice the width of the others, with all the load concentrated on points distributed with almost the accuracy of an engineer. The interior order—i.e., arcade, triforium, and clerestory—holds still by the somewhat dull mechanism of early Norman work, and the three elements are too nearly alike in vertical height for a result either beautiful or structurally significant. It lacks rhythm and subtlety of composition. The shaft-scheme of such transitional work as Noyon holds here, with cylindrical columns in the arcade supporting multiple shafts above, the vaulting shaft resting directly on the capital of the arcade column—an inorganic device much admired by Gothic theorists of the nineteenth century. On the other hand, the little Lombard round window has blossomed into the "Mystic Rose," which here approaches sublimity, and is used as the central feature of the terminations of nave and transepts. The whole nave is full of trials, experiments, changes, hurriedly adopted and half completed, and the exterior is marked by the same absorbing personality. In the chevet, for example, the mad and unbeautiful flying buttresses are not original; for at first the system was the subsequently standard type—two flights of arches, each properly grounded through pillar or wall-buttress. After a disastrous conflagration, however, some genius with a daring disproportionate to his discretion conceived the idea of covering both aisles with one enormous span. The result never commended itself, however, and is almost unique, but it shows at the same time the nemesis of structural pride that in the end, at Beauvais, was to close the history and the power over beauty of detail that was not mitigated by structural indiscretions; for the design of the buttress pinnacles of these

Brobdingnagian arches is perhaps the most beautiful single thing in Gothic architecture. As for the west front, it ever remains the great classical achievement of the Middle Ages, the most superbly conceived work of architecture that has ever issued from the hand of man in any place or at any time. It has no rival in the past, and none is conceivable for the future.

Laon was more or less contemporary with Paris, later if anything; but it is as different as may be. Where Paris is calm, serene, simple, Laon is nervous, complex, almost fantastic. For Paris two vast towers were enough, for Laon seven could hardly suffice. The whole work is tentative, vacillating, romantic, and, it must be confessed, inferior. Only in its conception and composition, however; in detail it is faultless, and one realizes here how, whatever the vagaries of the master-mason, the great body of artificers were always on hand to redeem primary mistakes by their conservative and assured taste and sense of beauty—a condition of things that in a sense marks the length of road we have traveled since then.

With Chartres, Bourges, and Rheims we come to a trinity of masterpieces that group themselves around the crowning years of Catholic civilization and are its sufficient expression and—if this

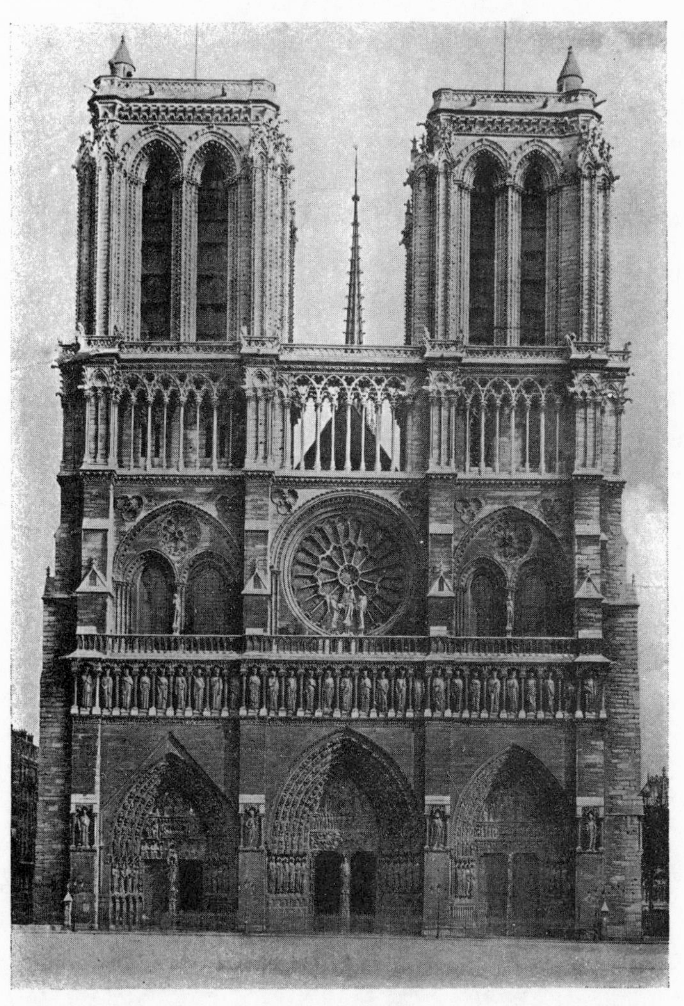

NOTRE DAME, PARIS (Plate X from *L'Art gothique en France*)

were needed—justification. Chartres dates in the main from 1194, when it was begun anew after a fire that destroyed all but the crypt and the west front, to 1260, when it was consecrated. In plan it is perhaps the noblest of all Gothic churches, while its interior, in point of organism, proportion, relation of parts, articulation, has few rivals. It is, I believe, the most perfect religious interior man has produced, as Paris is the greatest exterior, so far as its façade is concerned.

Bourges was begun in the same year with Chartres and its essential organism then determined, though the west bays of the nave were not completed until the very end of the thirteenth century. Its plan is wholly different from those of Paris, Laon, and Chartres (for there was then no copying of one master-builder by another) and its interior organism is quite original. It has no transepts and therefore no crossing, while its arcade is twice as lofty in proportion as the arcades of its sister-churches. It is the most aspiring and romantic of all and in some respects is the most brilliant in its artistic invention.

Rheims began to rise from its ashes in the year 1211, just when the savage tribes of Prussia began to yield to Christian missionaries—the last of the heathen races of North Europe to accept Christianity for a time—later to overwhelm in the red ruin of shell and flame the great church that in its building marked the moment of their evanescent conversion. The west front, to the base of the upper story of the towers, was finished with the close of the century. In plan, in exterior and interior organism, in detail, and in sculpture, Rheims was the perfected work of the Catholic civilization of the Middle Ages. Every other building shows here and there experiment, uncertainty, an almost nervous reaching out of its creators toward a dim ideal that was yet the one reality. Of this there was nothing in Rheims. It was the work of a master so supreme in his artistry that he laid hold on perfection where his followers struggled toward it. I am not sure that this perfect attainment raised it very far above Chartres or Bourges or Coutances. Final it was, in conception and in every minutest part, but to me there is something in the tremulous daring of Bourges, in the unsatisfied but eager desire of Paris, in the rapt faith and awestruck groping for the hand of God in Chartres, that appeals with a poignancy that in Rheims yields to dumb reverence for final and almost superhuman achievement. After all, man is the creature that *tries*, and in the striving for perfection we do not look for success; we resent it, in a sense, when one approaches it too closely. The great churches of the thirteenth century tried, as man tries, to achieve the unattainable, and in their failure they are sublime. One achieved, or almost achieved—Rheims—and, while we gave it the tribute of awed veneration, our hearts went first to the more human monuments of men, rather than of demigods. Rheims almost achieved the unattainable; its martyrdom has completed what its makers just failed of attaining, and for the future in the hearts of this and every succeeding generation, *in saecula saeculorum*, it will stand first in mind and in heart as the perfect work of man when he wrought in the fear of God.

Ten years after the beginning of Rheims the first stones were laid of Amiens, which progressed slowly through the century, the west towers being finished in the last quarter of the fourteenth century. Wonderful as the church is, with its perfectly developed chevet and dizzy nave, its exquisite carvings, and its masterly sculptures, it is the first evidence of the swerving of the thirteenth-century builders toward self-confident science and away from a purer artistic impulse. It is too competent, too perfect in its balancing of thrusts, in its concentration of loads, in the sumptuous decorations of its west front. It is true that it suffers bitterly from lack of the glass that glorifies Chartres and Bourges, and once was the crown of Rheims, but even this could not quite have blinded one to the consciousness that constructive intelligence was beginning to take the place of aspiration and inspiration, of joy in design and mastery of workmanship, of the divine ardor that lifted the tall arches of Bourges and made of the porches of Chartres and of the doors of Rheims masterpieces equaled only, if at all, on the Athenian Acropolis.

The choir of Le Mans is contemporary with Amiens and has the same merits and the same defects, at once the most ingenious and highly articulated in its chevet construction, and touched everywhere with the too perfect accomplishment of the structural engineer. Ten years after Amiens the choir of Beauvais was begun, and this was finished, with the crossing and spire, in 1274. Man already had accomplished more than he could rightly claim for his own. Here he tried for still more and failed; for twelve years later the spire and vault, which had been raised higher than Amiens and on more slender supports, fell in ruins, and though the choir was later rebuilt, with added reinforcements, the crossing tower was never reconstructed. The tran-

LAON CATHEDRAL—WEST FRONT

septs were built in the fifteenth century, and beautiful as they are, it is the beauty of the artist in ornament, not of the creator of an almost living organism, such as Chartres or Rheims.

With the close of the thirteenth century all the great work had been accomplished in France, where it had begun two centuries before. In the end man strove to attain by reason what is granted only to faith and prayer, and, as always happens in such circumstances, disaster followed close. After this only two things were possible: the freezing of tradition into that cold mastery that produced such correct and imposing monuments as St. Ouen and Cologne, or the wandering off into the wilderness of exuberant fancy and lawless fantasticism from which emerged the sumptuous front of Rouen and the impossible jewel-work of Brou.

I have taken a few churches from France alone to use as examples of the perfection of Catholic art. Of course the result is partial only, but it is impossible to concentrate in an hour the products of the two greatest centuries in history and to give some hints as well of the vital impulse that brought them into existence. One cannot know Gothic art as a whole without full regard for its manifestations in Great Britain—or Spain, or Flanders, or the upper

Rhine, for that matter—for this art was one; it reached from the Mediterranean to the Firth of Forth, and from the Danube to the Atlantic. There is no justification for those who see in it only certain new and consummate structural inventions and devices and so try to confine the name to masonry structures covered by ribbed and pointed vaults, or to those where the system of balanced thrusts is perfectly adhered to. Gothic is a spirit, as well as a mode—more than a mode—the spirit of a triumphant and universal Catholic culture; and you can make of it no less, as you cannot make of it more.

In Great Britain this culture was peculiarly deep and compelling, and its art therefore is of the noblest order, from Glastonbury through the whole wonderful sequence of Salisbury, Westminster, Lincoln, York Abbey, Guisborough, Gloucester, and the chapel of Henry VII, where it ends at last as French Gothic ended in Rouen and the transepts of Beauvais. In France the work was episcopal, communal, and secular; in England it was largely—and the best of it—monastic, which gives it a quality all its own and invaluable in its record of the nature and the influence of this greatest of mediaeval agencies for the spreading of culture and civilization. In

France, again, the triumphant work is that of the vast communal cathedrals; in England it is not only of the almost equally vast abbeys, it is even more especially of the myriad little parish churches which developed a character and a personality peculiar to themselves, equaled nowhere else, and as perfect in their way as the overwhelming glory and majesty of Bourges or Notre Dame.

France and England are the two great centers of mediaeval art expression, and France and England were the two countries where mediaeval culture reached its point of perfect development. In almost every other part of Europe we find, however, Gothic architecture, and in certain directions, as in painting, greater results than were achieved among Franks and Anglo-Saxons. There is a very noble early Gothic in Spain, and there also, and in Flanders, Italy, and the Rhineland, an art of later mediaevalism that is exquisitely beautiful in its combination of delicacy and opulent fancy. In every case it is tinged with a strong and vital nationalism, differentiating itself from the art of every other land, yet invariably true in essentials and in spirit to the great unity that, in spite of minor wars and rivalries, bound Europe together as never before or since.

From the beginning of the fourteenth century signs of decline showed themselves in architecture, but in all the other arts the advance was almost feverish in its intensity, particularly in poetry and painting and letters; and even in the failing architecture the loss was recorded rather in the great cathedrals and churches than in the minor productions of castles and civic halls and dwellings. Until a few months ago eastern France and Belgium were glorious with the splendid works of a culture still dominant in the fifteenth and sixteenth centuries, though now they are embers and ashes, after having been granted immunity by the contending armies of three centuries.

And this art continued in all its manifold phases until the Reformation, when, the impulse that had lasted for fifteen generations being withdrawn, it ceased almost in a day, and, except in music and poetry—and spasmodically in painting—has never been restored, though five other centuries have passed, clamorous for art, insistent in its practice, ignorant of how it was to be attained.

If we look for the secret of this strange and compelling art, we find it (as I have tried to show) in the unique culture of the time, which was the result of a triumphant and universally accepted

BEAUVAIS CATHEDRAL—SOUTH TRANSEPT

religious faith, a philosophy that supplemented instead of denying it, a just estimate of comparative values (strikingly unlike our own), and an industrial and economic system that may have lacked the earmarks of what we are pleased to call civilization, but produced fruits of character which the latter sometimes fails to reveal.

There was, we must always remember, but one faith and one Church, and these were not, as now, divided into an hundred inimical camps and accepted as accessories to a dominating life constituted on lines essentially antagonistic. Religion was the prime consideration, the one great reality, the personal possession of every man, and the Church was the concrete fact that made religion operative. Everywhere was a perfectly organized monasticism, more pervasive even than the secular priesthood, and every monastery was a center of culture, of education, and of order. With a very remarkable communal spirit went equal individuality, liberty, and independence. Capitalism was unknown, labor controlled its own destinies as it never has succeeded in doing since, and the guild system produced a condition of industrial vigor and efficiency that guaranteed a great measure of justice.

It would be impossible to exaggerate the importance of the guild system in connection with the quality of the work produced. The Greek workmen were slaves under a group of highly specialized experts; the Romans, slaves also, subject to the orders of a superior type of freedmen who were employed by their masters as we employ milliners and decorators; the mediaeval artificers were free citizens strengthened by co-operative association, and each man was in himself an artist, granted the independence of action due to such, and working under a powerfully fostered impulse of emulation that is the particular *bête noire* of the trade unions of today. There was no such thing as an architect, superior and supreme. An architect, as we count him today, is a sign of inferior culture, necessary but regrettable. There were master-workmen then, but each was simply *primus inter pares*, inspiring and co-ordinating, but leaving to his fellows their just share in invention and their free field for creative effort and aesthetic expression.

Behind the vitalizing power of religion and the stimulus of free expression lay certain immemorial traditions that undoubtedly reached back through the mysterious Comacini, with their traditions of symbolism and of mystic signification in numbers and forms and their relations, together with those that controlled the variations, irregularities, and refinements in the plan and in the vertical elements of a building. This whole question of symbolism and structural refinements is as baffling as it is fascinating. There is no longer room for questioning the existence of these things, and we owe much to the persistent investigations of Professor Goodyear, which have finally demonstrated the premeditated quality of the universal irregularities that reveal themselves in all the best of the buildings of the Middle Ages. The rationale of this strange subtlety is still to be found, but the thing itself is there, and it possibly reaches back through different races and nationalities at least to the time of the building of the Temple in Jerusalem, and it is as certainly one of the great elements in the perfect beauty of mediaeval work.

To this ancient and almost prehistoric form of tradition was added all the peculiar quality that grew out of the religion of Christianity, and while we need not accept the mystical and exaggerated theories of Huysmans, we must admit that there is in all mediaeval work a great mystery of symbolism and structural refinement, of which we ourselves know nothing; for with the coming in of capitalism after the close of the Middle Ages, the workman and craftsman became slaves again, the secrets all were lost, the sequence of tradition destroyed, and we are now left naked to the tender mercies of the architect, the general contractor, and unionized labor.

I have already spoken of the contributory part played by all the other arts in the great result, of the revitalized old arts of sculpture and painting and music, of the new arts, such as stained glass. In point of fact, it is wrong to use the word "contributory"; for it was not a case of many arts united to one end, it was rather *one art*, as one and indivisible as the Catholic religion and the Catholic Church, expressing itself in many ways and through different types of artists. With the Renaissance this unity was broken, art split up into as many followings as there were theological heresies during the Reformation, and no steps have been taken toward restoring that unity again. Art today is in the condition of Germany after the break-up of the Empire, a hundred little piffling states, none knowing where it was or what it existed for, and with no co-ordination and no sense of unity. As there, at times, through the whim of fate, some margrave or grand duke or elector was born greater than his kind, who gave for a moment a sudden splendor to his little state, so now, in any one of the arts, may arise, and does arise, a

LINCOLN CATHEDRAL—EAST END

genius who spreads a temporary glory on his little art, as Wagner or Browning or Richardson or St. Gaudens or Sargent; but each passes, and his art returns again to its normal level of mediocrity and general aimlessness.

Is there any possibility of recovery, of the finding again of the great aim that restores the vitalizing spirit, that unites art once more with many methods but one end? The art we have been considering gives the answer, the conditions now existing for half a year the opportunity. Civilization, our civilization, without culture and without any adequate sense of comparative values, has broken down in universal and cataclysmic war. It is no war of wilful kings or conscienceless diplomatists; it is no war without excuse and without reason for existence. Inevitable, unescapable, it involves the world with the grim fatalism that brought the universal Empire of Rome to its most timely end. When the culture of the Middle Ages was overwhelmed by the civilization of the Renaissance, certain tendencies were initiated that were bound to work themselves out to their logical conclusion. They have done so, and the perfect climax reveals itself in that region of Europe, and under the direction of that people, which last of all surrendered its heathenism to Christianity, but too late to acquire the everlasting benefits of the Middle Ages. On all the nations of the earth has come a great fear, for they see now what they themselves have made, and the evil and dark wrong it has produced. This is the great war between civilization and culture, between—as has been said—Corsica and Galilee, between the triumphant Renaissance-Reformation and a recrudescent mediaevalism.

Where the victory will rest is no question for argument; the answer is foreordained. Already the great and efficient system of modern civilization has over-passed its term and it must yield to something older and better, to that opposing culture which is the everlasting enemy of *Kultur*, a culture made up of that religion which is true because it is revealed by God, that philosophy which supplements religion instead of denying it and adapts its spiritual and mystical content to the limited and finite human intelligence, that art which is the harmonizing of both and their perfect and divinely ordained expression.

The new-found art of mediaevalism has revealed to the world the possibilities and the significance of art at its highest; it has led us back to the discovery of the comprehensive, stimulating, and character-building culture behind it. Through these things we can gain an answer to the appalling question forced on us by the Great War, seeing now the true nature of the civilization that could have issue in such a thing as this, realizing where, in spite of official "papers" of whatever color, right rests, and wrong, and finally realizing the lines on which, once the purging of the world is over, the new era must be built if the beneficent and regenerating culture of true religion, sound philosophy, and vital art is to return to a wasted but repentant and regenerate world.

The study of mediaeval art and mediaeval culture is not, at this time, a trivial playing with archaeology. It is the finding of the answer to the great question propounded by a world at war.

PRINCIPLES OF ARCHITECTURAL COMPOSITION

and

MODERN ARCHITECTURE

BY

THOMAS HASTINGS

III

PRINCIPLES OF ARCHITECTURAL COMPOSITION

Composition is not a subject for systematic analysis. We may learn about it in the lecture-room and by reading books, but in this way we can never acquire the art of composing. As in the case of the painter or sculptor, the architect must be apprenticed. Mere work never made an artist; a great work was never produced without great working. A man can never be a great artist without great industry. The extraordinary amount of work done, and well done, by the great masters in art—work which has survived—is incomprehensible to the modern artist. A man may think that he must wait for a so-called inspiration; but the real artist will find something to do for every hour and leave inspiration to take care of itself. Inspiration will come oftener, and with greater power, when the artist works without waiting for it.

Let us undertake less and work more. The mere direction of a number of draughtsmen to do our work for us is not art. As soon as the architect gives up the T-square and triangle and only directs others, he no longer advances, but retrogrades by this method of trying to manufacture architectural designs. Nor is it honest for an architect to pretend to be the author of work that others are doing for him, any more than it would be for a painter, a sculptor, or a writer to take credit for work he has not done.

There are many principles upon which the architect works and many laws which guide him in his study which it would be impossible to formulate, because he knows them intuitively. There are many vital things in the art of composition, just as there are in our everyday life, which are none the less true because we know them by intuition. The fact that we cannot formulate these things does not make them in any sense the less real. It is also just as true that there are many things in art which can be learned only by instruction and in which it will not do to trust to intuition. A proper instruction in these things will quicken and develop the intuition.

The most difficult thing in composition (and I believe this to be true of all art) is to know how to be simple, but to be simple without being stupid and colorless; to be firm and strong without being hard and angular; to have good detail, which, on the one hand, does not assert itself to the injury of the ensemble, and, on the other hand, is not timid for fear of a want of refinement. When a man has acquired a certain knowledge of his art, timidity is almost as bad as vulgarity and weakness as unpardonable as coarseness.

The highest logic in art is truth. It is neither logical nor true to have a great auditorium or principal room running through three or four stories of a building without some indication of it in the façade. If you are anxious to introduce into a composition a tower, a dome, or even an insignificant feature where the practical conditions imposed upon you will not allow you to expose such a motive in plan, do not build the motive, but do something else rather than resort to deceit or constructive trickery. If we only knew how to compose, the more variety offered us in the conditions imposed the more interesting would it be to look for the artistic solution of the problem. It is right to be logical; but a work of art was never beautiful solely because logical. There is no one who does more harm than the mere purist who worships what he thinks logic, but what is only prejudice, while he is blind to the fact that he is admiring and encouraging falsehood and vice in art and trampling truth under foot.

The more fertile the imagination of the composer the more carefully should he train his judgment, so that he will know what does not look well in his own work with as much facility and readiness as he would know what does not look well in the work of those associated with him. He must be his own impartial judge. A bad idea suppressed is a triumph for the good.

There seem to be two mistaken tendencies in our American methods of architectural education. The one class of men with whom we have to contend includes those who would dispense with the triangle, compass, and T-square, and with such familiarity with the orders and the principles of composition as will enable the student to use them with the utmost facility. They neglect these things, forsooth, to make room for what they call clever sketching. These men seem to have a peculiar disdain for the legitimate means of study, as though they were inartistic. The other class of men includes the pretended "savants" who would learn their profession as though a good knowledge of the history and literature of their art, with a course of general lectures, were all-sufficient, if followed by a few years of practical office experience.

To these so-called "savants," or the men who would teach architecture only in scientific or

GIRALDA TOWER AND CATHEDRAL, SEVILLE

literary ways, it should be said that architecture is an art rather than a science, and that when the architect is most skilled in his art he has least need of recourse to science. Of course, an architect must be familiar with descriptive mathematics for the purpose of calculating the intersection of vaults and roof, and for various problems in stereoptomy; but if the floor-plan has been well studied from an artistic or aesthetic point of view, there will rarely be left other difficult engineering and mathematical problems for the architect to solve. Here is the key to the entire problem.

All good composition begins with the thorough study of the plan. Few seem to realize that the floor-plan is anything more than a mere matter of the convenient arrangement of the several parts of the building. A good floor-plan, as seen on paper, has proportion, form, scale, color, values, and character; or it may be clumsy and inelegant. It determines the relation to each other of two of the three dimensions in space. It involves and determines the entire composition; the silhouette or outline of the whole structure is really projected on the plane of this drawing.

Not only does the silhouette or outline of the elevation in every sense depend upon the plan, but the best kind of perspective of it is here implied, because we can see therein the position and relative size of the different parts. When the plan is well studied, then it constructs well, builds well, and we need very little of analytical mathematics to assist us in our construction.

Until modern times, how much mathematics besides geometry and the descriptives did architects know, as compared with what we are given to learn, and what did they know of the strength of materials? With them it was mostly a question of good judgment with a proper and uncommon understanding of constructive principles and of stereoptomy, and the other descriptive mathematics. Analytical mathematics is comparatively a modern science. While there existed graphical rules for the approximate determination of the thrusts from arches as early as the thirteenth century, yet it practically is only in the past fifty years that the correct principles of constructive analysis have been fully developed; and there is still room for improvement in this direction. Until recently architects probably never calculated the strength of their materials or the thrust of arches and vaults. With them it was a question of intelligence, and not of ingenuity. It was the qualitative rather than the quantitative principles of construction that they studied, and these were always based upon experiment or experience. It was by knowing how to avoid difficult problems, with art in the floor-plan, that they escaped having difficult analytical problems to solve. We must always give precedence to practice before laws and theories.

If you were to show me a well-studied plan for the first time, I should not hesitate to say because of its beautiful proportions and the ability of its design that there is absolutely no necessity of calculating the thrusts of the arches and the strength of materials, excepting for the purpose of verification. In a well-studied floor-plan there will almost always be artistic reasons for making a pier economical in size and strong enough to support the weight that it has to carry. By pure mathematics we can determine only approximately what should be the size of a pier. The strength of materials must be estimated. We select at random several specimens of the stone to be used in our building. We obtain crucial tests for this purpose, and so we are supposed to learn from these few specimens the average weight per cubic inch which the stone will support. This we call our coefficient of strength in the stone chosen for our building. Taking into account the fact that the quarry where the stone is obtained may have a great fissure running through it, or may have other imperfections, the mathematician enters upon his calculations to learn how large a pier built of this stone should be to support the weight that is to be above it. After this the architect practically admits the inexactitude of his premises by increasing two or more times the size of the pier, and calls this the factor of safety or ignorance. I believe in such calculations for purposes of verification, but, in general, the piers will be about as safe to build upon when studied by an educated architect as when calculated by engineers.

It is really architecture and well-proportioned masonry versus engineering and iron girders. Each has its use, but they are not interchangeable. Buildings have stood *for centuries which were constructed without a knowledge of modern engineering*, solely because their plans as seen on paper were so well studied, so thoroughly artistic and beautiful, that constructive difficulties were avoided.

Now that photographs and illustrated books are so accessible to the student, copying or adaptation is a greater temptation than ever before. We compile more than we compose; but if our plan is first thoroughly studied to meet the practical requirements of the problem in hand, then when interpreting this plan and designing the façade we can neither copy nor adapt. Copying destroys progress in art and all spontaneity.

So long as a great many inartistic buildings are put up, the mathematical verification is needed for the protection of human life. Of course, there is one most unfortunate condition imposed upon us in these days, under which condition the plan has but a very small part to play in the solution of the problem—the so-called skyscraper. Here all would agree that expert mathematicians and engineers should be called in consultation, just as they are called in for questions of steam heating, ventilation, or electrical work. But even here great economy might obtain if with art the plan is so subdivided as to permit of a good distribution of weights and as much repetition as possible in the lengths of steel beams and girders. In monumental architecture the thicknesses of walls and piers should be proportionately related to the spans of the arches or to the distances and floor spaces. The thickness of a column should be proportioned to the intercolumniation, or distance between columns.

Do not misunderstand me. I would not disparage the thorough study of the plan from a utilitarian point of view. This is, in fact, the principal channel through which our life and habits can influence our composition and style. Before beginning to study the general composition of the floor-plan, it is first necessary to reduce the problem to its simplest form from a utilitarian point of view, taking into account the number of the principal rooms or divisions and the use to which they are to be put, their sizes, and the most reasonable form that should be given them. This is, as it were, the theorem or the program of the composition. If the question of disposition is not thus thoroughly understood at first, it will arrest the freedom of the mind and the imagination.

When a plan has been well studied, then in developing the exterior or interior few changes will be needed, even in details. In the further development of the scheme we need only fill our minds and hearts with the spirit, the ideas, and the sentiments of our age, and study to interpret the plan, in order to reach the best results.

Of equal importance is the question of the position or site of the building and the principal points from which it will be seen. Certain distributions of the several parts of the building that would be well for a low and flat country would be inappropriate for a hill. The streets,

CATHEDRAL AND GIRALDA TOWER, SEVILLE

promenades, or squares, or possibly water—river, lake, or sea—should of necessity have a great influence upon this distribution. The architect should know how to dispose his masses and should calculate upon the different effects with these conditions of environment taken into account. The plan which does not satisfy all such given conditions is not only impracticable, but must in consequence thereof be absolutely inartistic; for a good building must have obvious adaptation, both to its uses and to its environment. A plan has what we call good circulation when it is so arranged or composed that there is direct and easy communication between its different parts.

In general, it may be said that there are three kinds of floor-plans: the regular, the irregular, and the picturesque. A monumental floor-plan is almost always regular, unless the peculiarities of the site, or requirements, make this impossible. The regularity consists in the plan's having one principal axe. The irregular plan is an adaptation to the imperatives of an irregular site. It secures as much symmetry in the arrangement of its parts and proportions as the limitations of the site permit. The picturesque plan is not merely eccentric or lawless, but it is an attempt to conform to the picturesque conditions of the environment—at the same time preserving as much of symmetry in its details as such adaptation will allow.

For the sake of contrast the length of one room is ofttimes at right angles to the length of another room. This law of contrast is dominant in all art, and nowhere is the recognition of this law more important than in the design of a floor-plan. In general, the distribution of the rooms and the relation they bear to each other, also the thickness of the walls and the way they compose with each other, must give an interesting interior and exterior.

An architect delights in the study of a great plan—St. Peter's, for example. The original conception of this plan was Bramante's. With many elements of greatness, his design looked weak and proved to be weak. After his death there were thirty-three years of misfortune and accidents, though Guiliano di San Gallo, Vignola, Peruzzi, and others did some good work in trying to modify and improve Bramante's design. Then Michelangelo began by destroying the greater part of what had been done and gave us most of the plan as we now see it: namely, that part which directly supports and encompasses the dome. About one hundred years after Bramante's death Maderno added to

Michelangelo's work, which was in the form of a Greek cross, extending the nave and changing the plan to the form of the Latin cross. This addition is inferior to all the rest of the work. To this part of the building belongs the present façade, which is not worthy of the rest of the structure. It was a most unfortunate thing for Maderno that his work should be handed down to posterity between that of Michelangelo and that of Bernini, who planned the splendid colonnade and galleries in the front of the building. Without further reference to its history, looking at the plan as a whole, we all feel that it is a great building. This plan as an original work is one of the greatest ever conceived by the genius of man. Study the colonnade and galleries. The direction of the Vatican stairs, or the Scala Regia, on the right side of the church, is not at right angles to the façade. Bernini skilfully planned the straight portion of the galleries in axe with these stairs, and then, in order to symmetrize, he made the other gallery to correspond with it. It was of more importance to preserve the axes and symmetry than to have parallel lines. This arrangement not only made a more interesting silhouette, but it also made a better and more agreeable junction between the circular portion of the colonnade and the straight galleries. The forms of the piers at the two junctions are skilfully arranged, and they are charmingly repeated at the centers and extremities of the circular colonnade.

Again, think of the great Roman plans, the basilicas transformed into churches, the great Gothic cathedrals, and, in modern times, the Paris Opera House, the plan of which, without thought of the elevations, is the making of the building.

Having considered the plans of buildings, we might speak briefly of the plan of the immediate surroundings. We have a very characteristic name for this portion of the composition. We call it the "sauce of the architecture." It is this portion of the design which unites or marries the building with its natural surroundings or the landscape. Most of the same principles of composition obtain in the planning of this portion of the work as in the planning of the building itself. The architect should always have control of the design or plan of the immediate surroundings of his building.

If the site will allow it, the building should be so placed as to have the greater portion of the grounds on one side of it. This is very desirable, especially when the site is small in proportion to the size of the building. The object is to give a large and open space at least on one side, instead of a small frame or fringe all the way around the building.

It would seem as if this were merely common-sense, and yet how little is the principle recognized! How dreary are the suburban homes of the poorer classes in this country! It is mainly because a man, when he builds, places his small square house in the center of a square lot with a square walk around the house and a fence that forms a square around the walk; and, as if this were not enough, even the streets all form squares outside his lot.

While the landscape or surroundings should govern the general composition of the building in the beginning, the building should in turn, when completed, influence and govern the arrangement and composition of that portion of the landscape work which comes in immediate contact with it. This landscape work is to surround and to support the building, serving both as frame and as pedestal. The immediate accessories of the architecture, such as the terraces, balustrades, paths, fountains, or open spaces and vistas which come nearest the building, are really a part of the building itself.

While speaking of composition in plan, something should be said with reference to the general plan of cities, that is, the laying out of streets, avenues, or parks.

The plan of a city is rather an evolution than the work of an architect, and so gives precious testimony to the different phases of the life of the people. Many of the most interesting souvenirs of the past are seen in the general disposition of the streets and public squares. How much art, however, may be displayed in the influence of this evolution can be seen by looking at some of the cities of modern times. The greater portion of every city is the accumulated work of generation after generation. This development is determined by local circumstances, by the political constitution, and by the commercial and domestic life of the inhabitants. But happy is the city whose development in the cutting of new avenues and the building of new squares and parks has been governed or guided by men of thorough architectural training.

In this country, I feel that with the many good intentions in the appointment of federal commissions for the planning of the future development of cities, we architects have almost always undertaken too much and have been too ambitious in our planning. Such plans generally defeat themselves, and, alas, ofttimes frighten intelligent laymen. I know of several instances

CATHEDRAL AND CAMPANILE, FLORENCE, FROM OR S. MICHELE

where work has been either entirely abandoned or engineers have been employed and the architects disregarded. This is a great economic as well as practical mistake.

The plan, once determined and well studied, should suggest all it will in elevation and determine, in a way, all its component parts. Too much emphasis cannot be given to the thorough knowledge and understanding of the classic orders, especially the *Roman* orders—the foundations of all modern architecture since the Renaissance. In applying these classic orders to composition, we must remember that restraint is not bondage; it makes perfect freedom and progress possible, while slavish bondage ends every good work. Restraint does not destroy, but promotes, originality, guiding and stimulating it and opening the only safe paths which lead to usefulness and success.

In our American enthusiasm for Greek architecture we have too often lost sight of the greatness and nobility of the Roman school. The Greeks have never been surpassed in exquisite beauty of form and proportion, in extreme and subtle simplicity and refinement, or in the perfect harmony which pervades their every structure. They established the alphabet and rhetoric of all the true architecture which has come into the world since their time. It seems to me that most of their work was the outcome of each generation being content to improve the general composition bequeathed by the generation preceding, so as to make the temple, theater, or choragic monument a little better than ever before, thus coming so much nearer to perfection. When Ictinus built the Parthenon, we might almost say that the general composition was bequeathed to him. I would not for a moment say that it did not require just as high an order of genius to take the general composition which had been handed down and to make the Parthenon perhaps the most perfect and most intellectual monument ever built as it required to compose and originate the great dome of the Pantheon with scarcely a precedent leading up to it. This too was a great artistic achievement, perhaps never surpassed in the further development of domes. As if this were not sufficient in itself, it was probably the first great structure of this form on so large a scale that was ever built; and, in fact, the Romans and Etruscans were practically the originators of this mode of construction.

The Roman architect worked with independence and a singular self-sufficiency as a composer. His personality came to the foreground as he used this Greek alphabet and rhetoric to broaden out his work in more elaborate composition. Such buildings as the Baths of Caracalla, one of the finest plans ever made, the Pantheon, the Colosseum, the Basilica of Constantine, the several triumphal arches, and many other buildings, are not only great, but original, conceptions. What a splendid development the Romans made of the arch, both as a rational and a beautiful mode of construction! They were certainly *not an imitative people.* They did so much to make architecture meet more varied conditions of life that this brings them nearer to the still more varied conditions of today. Bramante, San Galo, Michelangelo, Paladio, Vignola, however, and all the great architects of the Renaissance, in every country, designed with the Roman orders for their classic standards.

There may not be a column or entablature in a building, but as long as there is a molding, a cornice, a window-sill, or an architrave, the architect will show in his work that he knows his orders and is familiar with their proportions and details.

Repetition is a governing principle. We Americans too often lose sight of this law for fear of being monotonous. A certain amount of monotony is a good thing, if we can get it in the right place and in the right way. What is there more beautiful and more impressive than a row of trees on either side of a straight country road! On the other hand, variety is another principle. It should always be characterized by order and symmetry and should be subservient to the ensemble of the composition.

Contrast in architecture is the bringing together of the two qualities or forms that are in opposition to each other, such as: simple wall surfaces with rich carving, light with shadow, a perpendicular line in contrast with a horizontal, a high story with a low story, a large opening with a small opening, a high and narrow opening with a broad and low opening. Contrast gives composition warmth and color; it is one of the salient characteristics of the Spanish Renaissance, and it is oftentimes found there in excess. Probably this is due to the influence of national character and climate.

The proper use of materials is to keep a true harmony between the design and the material in which it is to be executed, remembering that stone has to be cut; iron forged or molded; wood sawed, planed, or carved; while terracotta has to be modeled, molded, and baked. It would be useless for me to discuss how design must take into account the character of the materials to be used in construction. All of us know that a wooden column must be lighter than a stone one and an iron column much smaller than either, with sharper and more clean-cut moldings, all its members being drawn out longer and thinner. (These are the things that it is best not to theorize about too much, but to learn by practice.)

Perhaps the most important part of composition remains to be considered—namely, proportion and scale. In architecture, proportion is the mutual relation of the dimensions of the several parts of a building. For example, if an arch looks well, it is because there is a proper relation between its height and width. Good proportions practically depend upon a refined sense of what looks well and of what is in the highest sense harmonious with the purpose of the building. Vitruvius, Albert, and others have given certain systems of geometrical formulas to assist the architect in verifying or determining proportions, both in plan and in elevation. I believe that comparatively few artists have strictly adhered to any of them or have even taken many of them into serious account. There are certain principles of proportion which all must regard, but these principles cannot be reduced to formulas. The dimensions of a principal room or court which is not square or round—i.e., when it is a parallelogram—are ofttimes either double the width or equal to the diagonal of the square of the smaller side.

I believe that as a rule these geometrical formulas would hinder rather than help the imagination. There are certain relations that should exist between the diameter and the height of a column or between the height of a column and of the entablature and its intercolumniations. Again, such simple rules as that the height of an opening might be twice its width or that, under other circumstances, the height should be equal to the diagonal of the square of the smaller side, as in determining the proper proportions of an important room—such simple rules as these, modified according to circumstances, have always been accepted. The relation of one part of a building to another practically constitutes almost all that is beautiful in architecture. The relation of a column to the arch or wall in contact with it, whether over it, under it, or at one side of it, the relation of one story to another, of window openings to wall surfaces—these are all things, when we have new problems to solve, which, if they cannot be determined by the study of precedents, must be determined by that feeling

MILAN CATHEDRAL

and artistic judgment which come only with practice.

Men have become accustomed to seeing things done in a certain way, and, while this way cannot be formulated and is sometimes vague, we must conform to it wherever we can under our conditions. There is therefore a kind of unwritten law of proportion which only helps the architect and by which he need be limited no more than the painter or sculptor is limited in representing forms of nature. We are accustomed to seeing the human figure with certain proportions, and when we find in a drawing that these proportions are violated it shocks our sensibilities, not so much because such a deformity would not meet the conditions of existence, but because we are not accustomed to such proportions. The more the architect draws from both architecture and nature, the more quickened will his sensibilities be to distinguish what is good from what is bad. Conditions change or vary the proportions materially: for example, a column which has to support several stories must be heavier than one which is only decorative or which is on the upper floor, while a difference of materials would also require a change of the proportions. It is well known that a column which looks well with a wall behind it would look thin if it were to stand out against a clear sky. Thus a monument in the form of a single column surmounted by a statue is generally only six or seven of its diameters in height. Notwithstanding these variations, to meet exceptional conditions the true artist endeavors to keep a certain judicious equilibrium among all such variations. Much has been written about the necessity of altering the proportions of things which perspective foreshortens, or which are hidden in part by projecting cornices, or which will be seen from different points of view, in order to meet these different conditions. I believe that too much has been said upon this subject, and that, while there should be some accommodation to different conditions, there are not nearly so many required as one would think. An important thing to remember is that when any such accommodation is made, or when conditions are in any way taken into account, the final drawing of the elevation with the shadows cast must in every case have good proportions and look well.

A proof that a building which looks well in plan and elevation is almost sure to look well in execution or perspective is the fact that when we examine the measured elevations of great historical buildings, as given us in architectural books, we never see any distortion of any kind to remedy the effects of foreshortening, or any details increased in size so as to be out of proportion in the drawing because they are to be seen at a great height.

In general, the passer-by divines what projections conceal, because the shadows cast make him unconsciously estimate these projections. The mind works instinctively in making allowance for distances, just as we imagine the size of a ship or of a man seen in the distance. Thus the judgment rectifies illusions. Most of the exceptions are cases where a building has several surfaces in different planes, one surface coming behind another—for example, a tower rising behind a roof. Though the tower may need lifting to be seen, it would be a great risk to lift it so much that it does not look well in elevation. There must be an intelligent disposition of things and a proper method of carving or modeling the details according to the height for which they are intended rather than a changing of proportions or an enlargement of the ornament.

Closely allied to this question of proportion is what is known among architects as scale. This is one of the most subtle and indescribable things in all art. Proportion and scale are different things, though closely related. Proportion is the relation between the different parts of a composition; scale is the relation between the size of all these parts and an imaginary unit of measure which is determined by our sense of the fitness of things. This imaginary unit is fixed by our education, observation, and associations. To illustrate: we associate with a horse and a dog two different sizes. We might imagine a dog the size of a horse, and yet well proportioned; but he would be out of scale. One part of another animal might be out of proportion with the rest and yet not be out of scale; but one part out of scale would of necessity be out of proportion, if all the rest of the parts were not in scale with it. A horse's head may be ill formed, yet it may not be out of proportion; but if it is too large or too small, then it is out of scale and out of proportion also.

Experience and association demand a certain accord between the size of an object and its form. There is an intuitive demand in the minds of all men that the size of any object, though varying under different conditions, must correspond with the unchangeable things that surround it. The merit of a design should be such that it would not be consistent to increase or diminish any portion of the building, or even any detail.

The human figure is for the architect the unit of measure, because its normal or average size is most fixed upon his mind and because it was by man and for man that everything in architecture was originally conceived and developed. The height of a balustrade was for him to lean upon or to protect him; the size of a door for him to go through with comfort; the size of a building stone was for him to handle with convenience and reasonable facility; the size of a step was for him to mount. We might say approximately that in ordinary circumstances the balustrade should be about three feet high, the door not less than eight, the building stone from twelve to sixteen inches thick, the step six inches rise and twelve inches tread. Now, when these measurements meet the practical requirements they are right, not only from a utilitarian point of view, but also from an artistic point of view, and we speak of them as being in good scale or in scale with the rest of the building. The actual size in feet and inches of other things, such as columns, pediments, windows, cornices, arches, corbels, molding, ornaments, architraves, etc., has not been fixed by utility. The architect has acquired, by experience and association, a sense which determines the size as well as the proportions of these things, in order to make them appear in his building as they really are, without having to compare them with the size of a man standing by, for a unit of measure.

With the variation of the size of the building up to a given point, the number of parts or motives in the building itself need not necessarily change, but the relations that these parts have to each other and their respective proportions must change. To illustrate this principle: the normal man is larger than the dwarf, or the horse than the pony, but while in both instances the same features exist in each, their proportions are so different that in a photograph or an accurate drawing we can always distinguish the normal man from the dwarf or the horse from the pony. This is because in all four cases the characteristic features are in scale. This we feel either instinctively or by observation.

Now take an architectural example. There are certain buildings which do not look their real size. Instead of being impressed with the immensity of a building, we are surprised to find how small a man looks when we see him standing near it. That is because, while the proportions may be, in general, good, the building lacks scale. It could almost be said that it might be reduced to one-half its size, and without some definite

OSPEDALE MAGGIORE, MILAN—THREE WINDOWS

unit of measure to compare it with we should scarcely notice the reduction.

In building, all things are good in scale when they seem as large as they are. Bigness, for the sake of bigness, is small art. Often a small thing looks bigger than some big thing which looks small. If we err one way or the other, it is better to make a thing somewhat large in scale. Yet things that are large in feet and inches may be architecturally small. This entire question of scale is too often neglected and should always be given thought and careful study. Before beginning to work, it is well to sketch a man at one side of the paper, drawing him at the scale to be adopted. This is for comparison and guidance.

A large window and a large door look well if not exaggerated. A large arch or a large column in scale is imposing; if not in scale, it is ugly, and its bigness only emphasizes its ugliness. In general, when the size of a motive increases—as, for example, in a cornice—the number of its minor parts, such as moldings, should increase, though by no means proportionately with the increase of the cornice.

In our study, in order to understand fully the true conditions of things and the real proportions and the scale of our building, we should always blacken-in the walls of our plan, and draw and color-in the shadows of our façades and sections; otherwise we can never judge how the building will look in execution. This way of rendering drawings reveals the true proportions and conditions of things, while a perspective drawing distorts and misleads.

Though it is not universally the case, we can generally detect either one, two, or three clearly marked divisions in the height of a well-composed building. There is, as it were, a beginning, a middle, and an end in this vertical growth. Possibly this comes from the fact that nature itself seems to favor this triple division. We see it in space—length, breadth, and height; in time—past, present, and future; in the kingdoms—mineral, vegetable, and animal. We have always seen the triune in the aspirations and longings of men in ancient mythologies and religions, and in Christianity itself in its idea of the Trinity. There is a common tendency in writing to run one's adjectives in triads, for example: "He was honest, courteous, and brave"—a tendency which was very marked in Dr. Johnson. Dr. Holmes thinks that this comes of an instinctive and involuntary effort of the mind to present a thought or image with the three dimensions that belong to every solid, an unconscious handling of an idea as if it had length, breadth, and thickness.

We have so few well-composed buildings in the short history of American architecture that we have a right to expect from those who govern us such patriotism as will hold fast to the best as well as the time-honored landmarks of our national civilization. The historic monuments of a people may be regarded as the features of its countenance, through which is revealed the soul of that people. They should show respect for age. Our country has too few of these expressive lines of experience in its youthful historic countenance, and should have the soul to respect and save every one of them. It is perhaps not strange if, in the mad excitement of rebellion or revolution, men's passions lead them to destroy the very best of their own inheritance; but in times of peace, with calm and quiet deliberation to destroy the ancient landmarks which our forefathers have set for us—this seems utterly irreverent and inexcusable.

IV

MODERN ARCHITECTURE

We American architects are ofttimes confronted with the question why we have not an architecture of our own—one which is essentially American; and why it is that so many of us who have studied in Paris seem inclined to inculcate the principles of the École des Beaux-Arts into our American architecture. The majority of people do not seem to realize that in solving the problems of modern life the essential is not so much to be national, or American, as it is to be modern, and of our *own* period.

The question of supreme interest is: What influence has life in its different phases upon the development of architectural style? Style in architecture is that method of expression in the art which has varied in different periods, almost simultaneously throughout the civilized world, without reference to the different countries, beyond slight differences of national character, mostly influenced by climate and temperament.

Surely modern architecture should not be the deplorable creation of the would-be style inventors, the socialists who have penetrated the world of art farther than they have the world of politics, who are more concerned in promulgating an innovation than in establishing a real improvement—so-called Futurists, New Thinkers, Cubists, art nouveau followers, all unrelated to the past without thought of traditions. No more should modern architecture be the work of the illogical architect, living in one age and choosing a style from another, without rhyme or reason, to suit his own fancy or that of his client.

The important and indisputable fact is not generally realized that from prehistoric times until now each age has built in one, and only one, style. Since the mound-builders and cave-dwellers, no people, until modern times, ever attempted to adapt a style of a past epoch to the solution of a modern problem. In such attempts is the root of all modern evils. In each successive style there has always been a distinctive spirit of contemporaneous life from which its root drew nourishment. But in our time, contrary to all historic precedents, there is this confusing selection from the past. Why should we not be modern and have one characteristic style expressing the spirit of our own life? History and the law of development alike demand that we build as we live.

One might consider the history and development of costumes to illustrate the principle involved. In our dress today we are modern, but sufficiently related to the past—which we realize when we look upon the portraits of our ancestors of only a generation ago. We should not think of dressing as they did, or of wearing a Gothic robe or a Roman toga; but, as individual as we might wish to be, we should still be inclined, with good taste, to dress according to the dictates of the day.

The irrational idiosyncrasy of modern times is the assumption that each kind of problem demands a particular style of architecture. Through prejudice, this assumption has become so fixed that it is common to assume that if building a church or a university we must make it Gothic; if a theater, we must make it Renaissance. One man wants an Elizabethan house, another wants his house early Italian. With this state of things, it would seem as though the serious study of character were no longer necessary. Expression in architecture, forsooth, is only a question of selecting the right style.

The two classes with which we must contend are, on the one hand, those who would break with the past, and, on the other, those who would select from the past according to their own fancy.

CHATEAU DE BLOIS—AILE DE LOUIS XII—FAÇADE

Style in its growth has always been governed by the universal and eternal law of development. If from the early times, when painting, sculpture, and architecture were closely combined, we trace their progress through their gradual development and consequent differentiation, we cannot fail to be impressed by the way in which one style has been evolved from another. This evolution has always kept pace with the progress of the political, religious, and economic spirit of each successive age. It has manifested itself unconsciously in the architect's designs, under the imperatives of new practical problems, and of new requirements and conditions imposed upon him. This continuity in the history of architecture is universal. As in nature the types and species of life have kept pace with the successive modifications of lands and seas and other physical conditions imposed upon them, so has architectural style in its growth and development *until now* kept pace with the successive modifications of civilization. For the principles of development should be as dominant in art as they are in nature. The laws of natural selection and of the survival of the fittest have shaped the history of architectural style just as truly as they have the different successive forms of life. Hence the necessity that we keep and cultivate the historic spirit, that we respect our historic position and relations, and that we realize more and more in our designs the fresh demands of our time, more important even than the demands of our environment.

What determining change have we had in the spirit and methods of life since the revival of learning and the Reformation to justify us in abandoning the Renaissance or in reviving mediaeval art—Romanesque, Gothic, Byzantine, or any other style? Only the most radical changes in the history of civilization, such as, for example, the dawn of the Christian era and of the Reformation and the revival of learning, have brought with them correspondingly radical changes in architectural style.

Were it necessary, we could trace two distinctly parallel lines, one the history of civilization and the other the history of style in art. In each case we should find a gradual development, a quick succession of events, a revival, perhaps almost a revolution and a consequent reaction, always together, like cause and effect, showing that architecture and life must correspond. In order to build a living architecture, we must build as we live.

Compare the Roman orders with the Greek and with previous work. When Rome was at its zenith in civilization, the life of the people demanded of the architect that he should not only build temples, theaters, and tombs, but baths, basilicas, triumphal arches, commemorative pillars, aqueducts, and bridges. As each of these new problems came to the architect, it was simply a new demand from the new life of the people, a new work to be done. When the Roman architect was given such varied work to do, there was no reason for his casting aside all precedent. While original in conception, he was called upon to meet these exigencies only with modifications of the old forms. These modifications very gradually gave us Roman architecture. The Roman orders distinctly show themselves to be a growth from the Greek orders, but the variations were such as were necessary so that the orders might be used with more freedom in a wider range of problems. These orders were to be brought in contact with wall or arch, or to be superimposed upon one another, as in a Roman amphitheater. The Roman recognition of the arch as a rational and beautiful form of construction, and the necessity for the more intricate and elaborate floor-plan, were among the causes which developed the style of the Greeks into what is now recognized as Roman architecture.

We could multiply illustrations without limit. The battlements and machicolated cornices of the Romanesque, the thick walls and the small windows placed high above the floor, tell us of an age when every man's house was indeed his castle, his fortress, and his stronghold. The style was then an expression of that feverish and morbid aspiration peculiar to mediaeval life. The results are great, but they are the outcome of a disordered social status not like our own, and such a status could in nowise be satisfied with the simple classic forms of modern times, the architrave and the column.

Compare a workman of today building a Gothic church, slavishly following his detail drawings, with a workman of the fourteenth century doing such detail work as was directed by the architect, but with as much interest, freedom, and devotion in making a small capital as the architect had in the entire structure. Perhaps doing penance for his sins, he praised God with every chisel-stroke. His life interest was in that small capital; for him work was worship; and his life was one continuous psalm of praise. The details of the capital, while beautiful, might have been grotesque, but there was honest life in them. To imitate such a capital today, without that life, would be affectation.

Now a Gothic church is built by laborers whose one interest is to increase their wages and diminish their working hours. The best Gothic work has been done and cannot be repeated. When attempted, it will always lack that kind of mediaeval spirit of devotion which is the life of mediaeval architecture.

We might enumerate such illustrations indefinitely.

If one age looks at things differently from another age, it must express things differently. We are still living today in the period of the Renaissance. With the revival of learning, with the new conceptions of philosophy and religion, with the great discoveries and inventions, with the altered political systems, with the fall of the Eastern Empire, with the birth of modern science and literature, and with other manifold changes all over Europe, came the dawn of the modern world; and with this modern world there was evolved what we should now recognize as the modern architecture, the Renaissance, which pervaded all the arts and which has since engrossed the thought and labor of the first masters in art. This Renaissance is a distinctive style in itself, which, with natural variations of character, has been evolving for almost four hundred years.

So great were the changes in thought and life during the Renaissance period that the forms of architecture which had prevailed for a thousand years were inadequate to the needs of the new civilization, to its demands for greater refinement of thought, for larger truthfulness to nature, for less mystery in form of expression, and for greater convenience in practical living. Out of these necessities of the times the Renaissance style was evolved—taking about three generations to make the transition—and around no other style have been accumulated such vast stores of knowledge and experience under the lead of the great masters of Europe. Therefore whatever we now build, whether church or dwelling, the law of historic development requires that it be Renaissance, and if we encourage the true principles of composition it will involuntarily be a modern Renaissance, and with a view to continuity we should take the eighteenth century as our starting-point, because here practically ended the historic progression and entered the modern confusion.

Imagine the anachronism of trying to satisfy our comparatively realistic tastes with Gothic architectural sculpture or with paintings made by modern artists! Never, until the present generation, have architects presumed to choose from

TOURS CATHEDRAL

the past any style in the hope of doing as well as was done in the time to which that style belonged. In other times they would not even restore or add to a historic building in the style in which it was first conceived. It is interesting to notice how the architect was even able to complete a tower or add an arcade or extend a building, following the general lines of the original composition without following its style, so that almost every historic building within its own walls tells the story of its long life. How much more interesting alike to the historian and the artist are these results!

In every case where the mediaeval style has been attempted in modern times the result has shown a want of life and spirit, simply because it was an anachronism. The result has always been dull, lifeless, and uninteresting. It is without sympathy with the present or a germ of hope for the future—only the skeleton of what once was. We should study and develop the Renaissance and adapt it to our modern conditions and wants, so that future generations can see that it has truly interpreted our life. We can interest those who come after us only as we thus accept our true historic position and develop what has come to us. We must accept and respect the traditions of our fathers and grandfathers and be, as it were, apprenticed by their influence. Without this we shall be only copyists, or be making poor adaptations of what was never really ours.

The time must come—and, I believe, in the near future—when architects of necessity will be educated in one style, and that will be the style of their own time. They will be so familiar with what will have become a settled conviction and so loyal to it that the entire question of style, which at present seems to be determined by fashion, fancy, or ignorance, will be kept subservient to the great principles of composition which are now more or less smothered in the general confusion.

Whoever demands of an architect a style not in keeping with the spirit of his time is responsible for retarding the normal progress of the art. We must have a language if we would talk. If there be no common language for a people, there can be no communication of ideas, either architectural or literary. I am convinced that the multiplicity of printed books and periodicals written by literary critics and essayists who have not even been apprenticed but are writing with authority about art, has, perhaps, been more instrumental than anything else in bringing about this modern confusion. I believe that we shall one day rejoice in the dawn of a modern Renaissance, and, as always has been the case, we shall be guided by the fundamental principles of the classic. It will be a modern Renaissance, because it will be characterized by the conditions of modern life. It will be the work of the Renaissance architect solving new problems, adapting his art to an honest and natural treatment of new materials and of new conditions. Will he not also be unconsciously influenced by the twentieth-century spirit of economy and by the application of his art to all modern industries and speculations?

Only when we come to recognize our true historic position and the principles of continuity in history, when we allow the spirit of our life to be the spirit of our style, recognizing, first of all, that form and all design are the natural and legitimate outcome of the nature or purpose of the object to be made—only then can we hope to find a real style everywhere asserting itself. Then we shall see that consistency of style which has existed in all times until the present generation; then, too, shall we find it in every performance of man's industry, in the work of the artist or the artisan, from the smallest and most insignificant jewel or book-cover to the noblest monument of human invention or creation, from the most ordinary kitchen utensil to the richest and most costly furniture or painted decoration.

We must all work and wait patiently for the day to come when we shall work in unison with our time. Our Renaissance must not be merely archaeological—the literal following of certain periods of the style. To build a French Louis XII or Francis I or Louis XIV house, or to make an Italian cinquecento design, is indisputably not modern architecture. No architect until our times slavishly followed the characteristics of any particular period, but he used all that he could get from what preceded him, solving such new problems as were the imperatives of his position.

What did a man like Pierre Lescot, the architect of the Henry II Court of the Louvre, endeavor to do? It would have been impossible for him actually to define the style of his own period. That is for us, his successors, to do. For him the question was how to meet the new demands of contemporaneous life. He studied all that he could find in classic and Renaissance precedents applicable to his problem. He composed, never copying, and always with that artistic sense of the fitness of things which was capable of realizing what would be harmonious in his work. In the same way all architects, at all times, contributed to a contemporaneous architecture, invariably with modifications to meet new conditions. This must be done with a scholarly appreciation of that harmonious result which comes only from a thorough education. So, with freedom of the imagination and unity of design, an architecture is secured expressive of its time.

Again, as in all times until now, there will be design and not mere novelty in the carriage, automobile, or boat, as well as in the endless variety of implements of utility or amusement.

How is it with us in modern times? Not only do many architects slavishly follow the character of some selected period, but they also deliberately take entire motives of composition from other times and other places to patch and apply them to our new conditions and new life. Every man's conscience must speak for itself as to whether such plagiarism is right; but while the moral aspect of this question has very little to do with art, yet intellectually such imitative work, though seemingly successful, positively stifles originality, imagination, and every effort to advance in the right direction.

The way is now prepared for us to endeavor to indicate what are some of the principal causes of the modern confusion in style. With us

Americans an excessive anxiety to be original is one of the causes of no end of evil. The imagination should be kept under control by given principles. We must have ability to discern what is good among our own creations and courage to reject what is bad. Originality is a spontaneous effort to do work in the simplest and most natural way. The conditions are never twice alike; each case is new. We must begin our study with the floor-plan and then interpret that floor-plan in the elevation, using forms, details, and sometimes motives, with natural variations and improvements on what has gone before. The true artist leaves his temperament and individuality to take care of themselves.

Some say that if this is all that we are doing there is nothing new in art; but if we compose in the right way there can be nothing that is not new. Surely you would not condemn nature for not being original because there is a certain similarity between the claw of a bird and the foot of a dog, or between the wing of a bird and the fin of a fish. The ensemble of each creature is the natural result of successive stages of life, with variations of the different parts according to the principles of evolution. There are countless structural correspondences in the skeletons of organic life, but these show the wonderful

CHURCH OF ST. ETIENNE DU MONT, PARIS

unity of the universe; and yet, notwithstanding this unity, nature is flooded with an infinite variety of forms and species of life.

We must logically interpret the practical conditions before us, no matter what they are. No work to be done is ever so arbitrary in its practical demands but that the art is elastic and broad enough to give these demands thorough satisfaction in more than a score of different ways. If only the artist will accept such practical imperatives as are reasonable, if only he will welcome them, one and all, as friendly opportunities for loyal and honest expression in his architecture, he will find that these very conditions will do more than all else besides for his real progress and for the development of contemporaneous art in composition.

Never resent what at first thought may seem to be limitations and in despair try to change conditions which, if reasonable, should suggest new and interesting design. Frederick the Great said: "The great art of policy is not to swim against the stream, but to turn all events to one's own profit. It consists rather in deriving advantage from favorable conjunctures than in preparing such conjunctures." And when told of the death of the Emperor Charles VI, he said to a friend who was with him: "I give you a problem to solve: When you have the advantage, are you to use it or not?"

The architects in the early history of America were distinctly modern and closely related in their work to their contemporaries in Europe. They seem not only to have inherited traditions but religiously to have adhered to them. I believe that it is because of this that the genuine and naïve character of their work, which was of its period, still has a charm for us which cannot be imitated. McComb, Bulfinch, Thornton, Letrobe, L'Enfant, Andrew Hamilton, Strickland, and Walters were sufficiently American and distinctly modern, working in the right direction, unquestionably influenced by the English architecture of Indigo Jones, Sir Christopher Wrenn, James Gibbs, Sir William Chambers, and others. Upjohn and Renwick, men of talent, were misled, alas, by the confusion of their times, the beginning of this modern chaos, the so-called Victorian-Gothic period.

Gifted as Richardson was, and great as was his personality, his work is always easily distinguished, because of its excellent quality, from the so-called Romanesque of his followers. But I fear the good he did was largely undone because of the bad influence of his work upon his profession. Stumpy columns, squat arches, and rounded corners, without Richardson, form a disease from which we are only just recovering. McComb and Bulfinch would probably have frowned upon Hunt for attempting to graft the transitional Loire architecture of the fifteenth century upon American soil, and I believe that all will agree that the principal good he accomplished was due to the great distinction of his art and to the moral character of the man himself rather than to the general influence and direction of his work.

Whether we agree with Charles F. McKim or not in wanting to revive in the nineteenth century the Italian Renaissance of the sixteenth century, the art of Bramante, St. Galo, and Peruzzi, he had perhaps more of the true sense of beauty than any of his predecessors in American art. His work was always refined, individual, and had a distinctly more classic tendency in his most recent buildings.

We have seen that the life of an epoch makes its impress upon its architecture. It is equally true that the architecture of a people helps to form and model its character, in this way reacting upon it. If there be beauty in the plans of our cities and in the buildings which adorn our public squares and highways, its influence will make itself felt upon every passer-by. Beauty in our buildings is an open book of involuntary education and refinement, and it uplifts and ennobles human character. It is a song and a sermon without words. It inculcates in a people a true sense of dignity, a sense of reverence and respect for tradition, and it makes an atmosphere in its environment which breeds the proper kind of contentment, that kind of contentment which stimulates true ambition. If we would be modern, we must realize that beauty of design and line in construction build well, and with greater economy and endurance than construction which is mere engineering. The qualitative side of a construction should first be considered, then the quantitative side. The practical and the artistic are inseparable. There is beauty in nature because all nature is a practical problem well solved. The truly educated architect will never sacrifice the practical side of his problem. The greatest economic as well as architectural calamities have been performed by so-called practical men with an experience mostly bad and with no education.

It is, I believe, a law of the universe that the forms of life which are fittest to survive—nay, the very universe itself—are beautiful in form and color. Natural selection is beautifully expressed, ugliness and deformity are synonymous;

and so it is in the economy of life—what would survive must be beautifully expressed.

Has the world beheld in art that which we call style, changing with each age, the visible expression of man's inner consciousness, appearing above the horizon with the dawn of civilization, gradually developing in orderly sequence, one degree upon another, following the course of time? Has all this come into existence only to disappear again on the other side of the small circle of its horizon? Has history recorded its progress from dawn to twilight, unconscious of its rapid fading into the darkness of night? Or will it rise again, following the natural laws of the universe? Or, like the falling star, is it lost in the confusion of eternal space, never to appear again?

As each age tells its own story in its own language, shall we tell our story to future generations in our own way? A great tide of historic information has constantly flowed through the channel of monuments erected by successive civilizations, the art of each age being an open book recording the life and spirit of the epoch, ofttimes verifying the truth of its own literature, an integral part of the whole scheme of evidence. The archaeologist thus supplements the historian, but alas, with the chain divided, the future will have drifted away from the past into a vast ocean of discord, where architectural continuity will have ceased to exist.

The recently discovered buried cities of Assyria give us a vivid idea of the civilization lost to history. The Pyramid of Cheops and the temples of Karnak and Luxor tell us more of that ingenuity which we cannot fathom and of the grandeur and life of the Egyptian people than the scattered and withered documents or fragments of inscriptions that have chanced to survive the crumbling influences of time.

The Parthenon and the Erectheum bespeak the intellectual refinement of the Greeks as much as their epic poems or their philosophy. The triumphal arches, the aqueducts, the Pantheon, and the basilicas of Rome tell us more of the great constructive genius of the early republic and the empire of the Caesars than the fragmentary and contradictory annals of wars and political intrigues. The unsurpassed and inspiring beauty of the Gothic cathedrals which bewilder us, and the cloisters which enchant us, impress on our minds a living picture of the feverish and morbid aspirations of mediaeval times, a civilization that must have had mingled with its mysticism an intellectual and spiritual

APSE OF CHURCH OF ST. PIERRE, CAEN

grandeur which the so-called Dark Ages of the historian have failed adequately to record; and in America, even amid the all-absorbing work of constructing a new government, our people found time to speak to us of today in the silent language of their simple colonial architecture of the temperament and character of our forefathers.

And when in the tumult of this modern warfare men's passions overcome their reason, and the great monuments of history that have survived the ages are subjected to the onslaught of modern armament, let us hope that they may not be further subjected to the work of the architect who would fain restore them in the style which has passed and so rob us of all that is left. Let them be protected by every device from further destruction, to tell the story of this twentieth-century civilization, this vaunted culture which has failed to respect and protect its heritage.

Will our monuments of today adequately record the splendid achievements of our contemporaneous life, the spirit of modern justice and liberty, the progress of modern science, the genius of modern invention and discovery, the elevated character of our institutions? Will disorder and confusion in our modern architectural styles express the intelligence of this twentieth century? Would that we might learn a lesson from the past—that modern architecture, wherever undertaken, might more worthily tell the story of the dignity of this great epoch and be more expressive of our contemporaneous life!

ORGANIC ARCHITECTURE
and
THE LANGUAGE OF FORM

BY

CLAUDE BRAGDON

V

ORGANIC ARCHITECTURE

With the echoes of distant battles in our ears and in the face of economic and industrial problems which clamor for solution, it may seem the height of futility to discuss mere matters of aesthetics. It is not so, however, any more than it is futile to forecast the harvest even while last year's stubble disappears before the plough. Outworn social orders go down before the cannon and sword in order that mankind may realize new ideals of beauty and beneficence already existent in the germ.

It is clear that "the old order changeth," not alone in the House of Life, but in the Palace of Art. Anarchy clamors at that door too. In painting, in music, and in the drama we are entered upon that phase in which the bolder spirits are rejecting alike the passing fashions and the forms sanctified by time, and are seeking new generalizations. Architecture, the least plastic of the arts, lags a little; but the great unrest has seized that also.

We observe a great confusion of ideas upon the whole subject of architecture, not alone on the part of the public, but in the profession itself. Eminent architects are found to differ widely in their opinions, and these differences find expression in their work. It is clear that there is no common agreement among them as to what constitutes excellence. If we apply only the criterion of everyday common-sense, it would appear that the modern architect has not grasped the modern problem. Let me try to prove to you that this is so.

First, the architect of today fails to think and work in terms of his place.

A proof of this failure is found in the unsuitability of many commonly used architectural forms and features to practical needs and to climatic and environic conditions. Cornices, made for the etching of strong shadows and for protection from a tropic sun, frown down from the skylines of our cloudy northern cities, where they gather dirt and soot in summer and in winter become traps for snow and ice. Arcades and colonnades, originally designed for shade and shelter, rob overstrained eyes of the precious light of day. Expensive and useless balustrades protect waste spaces of roof where people could not take their pleasure if they would.

Secondly, the architect fails to think and work in terms of his time.

A proof of this failure is found in the perfectly meaningless character of the architectural ornaments in common use: the acanthus scroll, the egg and tongue, the Greek fret and waterleaf, the festoon and wreath, a cartouche, a shield, a lion's head—echoes all of the past, not one eloquent of the present.

Thirdly, the architect fails to think and work in terms of his materials.

A proof of this failure is found in the common practice of substituting one material for another —wood for iron, terra-cotta for stone, stone for concrete, or vice versa—by reason of their differences in cost, without essential modification in design. One of the most important functions of architecture is thus violated—the showing forth of the splendor and beauty (be it a beauty of strength or of fragility) of different materials, making the most of the unique characteristics of each.

Now the beauty of terra-cotta, for example, is not less than that of stone, but it is different. Witness a Della Robbia lunette and a carved granite Egyptian bas-relief. Imagine the terracotta arcades of the Certosa of Pavia carved in stone. One would fairly ache at the thought of so much labor and feel a sort of terror at so great a weight so insufficiently supported. On the other hand, were the heavily rusticated street front of the Pitti Palace in Florence translated,

ıge, from stone to terra-cotta, the be no less distressing, but for the ıson. There would be no charm of detail and texture to compensate for the splendid ponderosity of stone.

In the face of these facts, it will be well if we first of all find out exactly where we stand and what we are doing. Let us therefore try to get this clear without further loss of time.

Looking at the matter from the broadest possible point of view, it is evident that we dwell in a composite environment: that in which we find ourselves, Nature; and that which we make for ourselves, the product of industry and art. In this city of Chicago, for example, a wilderness of railroads, stockyards, houses, skyscrapers has obliterated the earlier wilderness of trees and swamp and prairie grass. Nothing so diametrically foreign to Nature as this gridiron plan and these rectilinear buildings could well be imagined. Man has himself essayed the rôle of creator and follows a different dream.

This has been the case more or less ever since the stern desire for mastery and the sweet disease of art disturbed the balance of Nature in men's souls. When we come to consider architecture throughout the world and down the ages, we find it bisected by a like inevitable duality: either it is *organic*, following the law of natural organisms; or it is *arranged*, according to some Euclidian ideal devised by proud-spirited man. In other words, it is either cultivated, like the flower; or it is cut, like the gem.

It is important that this fundamental difference in aim and method should be clearly perceived and thoroughly understood. This will be best accomplished by comparing and contrasting Gothic architecture, so-called, which is preeminently a striving toward a free organic expression of plan and construction, with Renaissance architecture, wherein predetermined canons of abstract beauty are imposed.

The popular conception of Gothic architecture is of a manner of building practiced throughout the north of Europe during the Middle Ages, the distinguishing characteristics of which were pointed arches, groined vaulting, buttressed walls, traceried windows, and the like. But if we study those principles of planning and construction which produced and determined the above-mentioned characteristics of the style, we might appropriately describe Gothic as a manner of building in which the form is everywhere determined by the function, changing as that changes. Renaissance architecture, on the other hand, represents an ideal in conformity with which the function is made to accommodate itself, to a certain extent, to forms and arrangements chosen less with a view to their exact suitability and expressiveness than to their innate beauty. In short, Gothic architecture is organic; Renaissance architecture is arranged.

These definitions, embodying the distinction noted, should not be taken to imply any disparagement of Renaissance architecture, that strained and triply refined medium through which some of the noblest strivings of the human spirit toward absolute beauty have achieved enduring realization. Arranged and organic architecture correspond to the two hemispheres of thought and feeling into which mankind is divided, the one pre-eminently intellectual, the other psychic. They represent fundamental differences of principle and ideal, unrelated to considerations of time and space.

In what, more specifically, do these differences consist? The basic one is that organic architecture, both in its forms and in the disposition of these forms, follows everywhere the line of the least resistance, achieving an effect of beauty mainly by reason of the fact that utility is the parent of beauty and that any increase in fitness is an increase in beauty.

In arranged architecture, on the other hand, this principle yields precedence to a metaphysical ideal of pure or abstract beauty, achieved by the employment of forms, rhythms, and arrangements, developed by a process of selection and survival, and having for that reason a less vital relation to the whole construction than in the case of Gothic architecture.

Organic architecture does not reject any form or any arrangement developed by long use and of acknowledged beauty, so long as it, as well as another, tells a given story or accomplishes a given end. As soon as it becomes inexpressive or inefficient, however, by reason of changed conditions, it is modified or rejected, or a new one is created; whereas in arranged architecture, forms originally organic survive even after they have lost their *raison d'être*. It was for this reason that the Romans employed the orders after they had developed the arch. To the devotee of arranged architecture, beauty is its own sufficient justification; to him who follows the organic ideal, as soon as a thing becomes false to the mind it ceases to be fair to the eye.

The spirit behind organic architecture is adroit, inventive, fertile, resourceful. It is economical of materials and means, even in its most sumptuous creations. It is most itself when engaged in attaining a given end in the simplest and most direct manner possible. It is given to short cuts and uses the tools and materials nearest to its hand. The great cathedrals are built of stones of easily manageable size, requiring no elaborate machinery. The spirit behind arranged architecture, on the other hand, disdains these considerations. There is a sublime arrogance in the way in which, to compass one of its grandiose effects, it spends money by millions and kills men like flies. The first seems to say to Nature: "Permit me, madam, to assist you; there is a final felicity which, with your permission, I shall add." And it does this quite in Nature's manner, without, so to speak, disturbing a hair of her head. The second says, rather, "I'll show you a trick worth two of that," and proceeds to obliterate the landscape and put something altogether different in its place. It is inconceivable, for example, that the Gothic builders would have converted a swamp into a pleasure garden, as Louis XIV, that prince of bromides, did at Versailles, at such enormous cost of lives and treasure. It is equally inconceivable that the architects of the Renaissance would have hung a church upon a crag, as the

PALACE OF VERSAILLES

mediaeval builders did at Mont Saint Michel—without, at least, leveling and terracing the crag.

In all true Gothic there exists so intimate a relation between the interior arrangement and the exterior appearance—between the plan and the elevation—that from a study of the latter the former may with fair accuracy be read. The manner of construction rules the whole structure and declares itself at sight. In Renaissance architecture, even at its best, this by no means follows; the elevation, determined by considerations of grandeur, symmetry, proportion, is often only a mask. St. Paul's Cathedral, in London, is an example of this. The buttresses of the arches of the nave are concealed behind a curtain wall surmounted by a balustrade which stands, independent of any roof, high aloft in the air. The stone lantern which crowns the dome appears to be supported by it, but the visible dome is of wood, a falsework which conceals the truncated cone of brickwork which alone saves the lantern from tumbling into the center of the church. This mendacity of the Renaissance spirit is one of its distinguishing characteristics. The application to a wall of columns and entablature, arches and imposts, which support nothing, not even themselves, is one of its most common and most innocuous forms. Some of these artifices are quite justifiable from the standpoint of mere aesthetics, as I shall endeavor to show in my second lecture; but the true Gothicist will have none of them, his motto being, "Beauty is Truth; Truth, Beauty."

In arranged architecture, the various parts and details are assembled and combined by the sovereign good taste of the architect; in organic, they are melted and fused by the creative heat, the eagerness for self-expression. In whatever form it appears, organic architecture seems to spring up without effort, almost of its own volition, a natural outcropping of national and racial vitality. Men do not have to learn to understand it; they recognize themselves in it because they carry the clue to its meaning in their hearts. Arranged architecture, on the other hand, is the self-conscious embodiment of the pomp and the pride of life. Like Little Jack Horner, it seems to say, "What a great boy am I!"

It is not profitable to multiply these distinctions, for this might lead more to confusion than to clarity of mind. It is necessary only to remember that the real point of cleavage between organic and arranged architecture is the one first dwelt upon. In order to determine to which hemisphere of expression a given building belongs

MONT-SAINT-MICHEL

it is necessary only to apply the acid test of Mr. Sullivan's formula and ask, "Does the form follow the function, or is the function made subservient to the form? Did the spirit build the house, or does the house confine the spirit?" If the first, it is organic; if the second, it is arranged.

Ponder this formula, then apply it. Strange truths emerge. It is plain from existing evidences, and from our knowledge of their psychology, that the Greeks built in the organic spirit, and that there is more real identity in principle between the Erechtheum, let us say, and the Saint Chapelle, than between the former and the most correctly classic building in all Paris. The Romans worked organically in the planning and construction of their vast and complicated basilicas, theaters, and baths; but they knew not where to stay their hand, and, seduced by a beauty which they did not comprehend, they meaninglessly applied the orders to their arch and vault construction—that is, they employed organic forms as mere ornament, after the virtue had flowed out of them by reason of a change of structural methods.

Turning the searchlight of our formula in different directions up and down the ages, we discern that the Church of Santa Sophia in

Constantinople is organic, for the reason that it consists of a single consistent system of construction—that of the round arch and spherical vault—carried to its logical development, nowhere hidden, everywhere expressed. The Houses of Parliament in London, on the other hand, with a whole bagful of Gothic tricks, are nevertheless arranged architecture. They are this for the reason that the elaborately composed river façade gives no hint of what lies behind it, and the towers might have been in one place as well as another, or not at all, so far as any necessity is concerned. In other words, the element of inevitability is lacking, that sure index of the organic spirit. Called upon to create a Gothic design, Sir William Barry, the architect, could change the clothing of his idea, but not the complexion of his mind.

It is held by those who have intimate knowledge of the curious architecture of Japan that the Japanese built organically in the carrying of wood architecture to the highest logical development that the world has ever seen. That Mr. Cram should himself be the author of a delightful and scholarly treatise on Japanese architecture is an eloquent fact in this connection.

SANTA SOPHIA, CONSTANTINOPLE

Coming again to the consideration of modern architecture here in America—barring a few thrice-blessed exceptions—it is certainly not organic, and to call it arranged would place it in the same category with the masterpieces of the Renaissance, which would be to pay it a higher tribute than it deserves.

Let us consider the main features of this architecture, if on the face of chaos features can be discerned. To consider modern architecture from the standpoint of structure presents no difficulty. Every important building of today adheres to substantially one method of construction. Even a layman knows its characteristic features: a steel framework, floors and roof of hollow tile or reinforced concrete, an outer covering of brick, stone, or terra-cotta, as the case may be. But when we come to consider the language in which the story is told to the beholder, there is the greatest confusion of tongues. Venetian palaces elbow French chateaux and Roman temples; pseudo-Gothic competes with neo-Greek, each masquerading as something other than it is—a Brobdingnagian saturnalia of vociferous unreason.

The cause of this discrepancy between the inner structure and its outward manifestation is not far to seek. The construction has been shaped by the living hand of necessity, and is therefore rational and logical; the outward expression is the result of the architect's "digging in the boneyard." There has been laid upon it the dead hand of the past. Free of this incubus, the engineer has succeeded; subject to it, the architect has failed. That is, he has not seen that the new construction imperatively demanded a new space-language for its expression. By limiting himself to the great styles of the past and the forms developed by superseded methods of construction, he has shown himself impotent to create for this great age an architecture eloquent of it. This is the manner and measure of his failure, and it is grave.

Now it is true that architectural styles are not created merely by taking thought of the matter, but grow imperceptibly, new conditions modifying old traditions. Conservatism in architecture is therefore a good and necessary thing, but in times like the present conservatism ceases to be a virtue. The architect who clings blindly to precedent in dealing with the unprecedented, as he is now constantly forced to do, is in the position of the boy who stood on the burning deck. This habitual attitude of looking backward at the past over the shoulder of the present,

HOUSES OF PARLIAMENT, LONDON

instead of fronting the future, has resulted for the architect in the atrophy of his creative faculty.

Of course, no architect can afford to dispense with a knowledge of his art as practiced throughout the world and down the ages. It is even well that he should train himself to think and work in terms of this style and of that, if only to learn that a style takes its form and characteristics from the materials and methods of construction employed, and its ornament from the racial and national psychology. From the history of architecture nothing is clearer than that a change of construction, or a change of consciousness, demands and finds fresh architectural forms for its expression. We of today use a kind of construction unknown to the ancients, and our psychology is different; yet we look about us in vain for a space-language which expresses both in terms of beauty. I use the term "space-language" because the time-language of today already exists or is in process of formation in the modern drama, the modern novel, and modern music—new art forms made to meet new needs of expression. The need is not less urgent for a new architectural language. It is bound to come in time. The question naturally arises: To which of the two hemispheres before mentioned will it belong; will it be organic or will it be arranged?

The answer to this question is probably involved in the answer to a more grave and vital question, one which the clouded and ambiguous aspect of the times cannot fail to suggest to every thoughtful mind. Putting aside all purely local and temporal issues, the great issue of the immediate future is between the forces of materialism, on the one hand, which work against the practical realization of human brotherhood, and those obscure spiritual forces which are working for it. If materialism triumphs—and materialism is as strongly intrenched in the hovel as in the mansion, in the church as in the market-place—architecture, however highly developed and perfected, will be the work of slaves for masters—*arranged* by master-minds. If, on the other hand, the spirit of democracy and of true brotherhood triumphs, architecture will become again *organic*, the ponderable expression of the truths of the spirit, wrought out in all humility and lovingness by those who are its subjects but not its slaves.

We are warranted in this conclusion by the history of art itself. Every organic architectural evolution followed in the wake of a religious impulse, and the ideal of brotherhood is the impulse which today moves men to those fervors and renunciations which have marked the religious manifestations of times past. If today we use, only to misuse, the architectural languages of the past, it is because materialism holds us and rules us; if tomorrow we are able to express ourselves in a language of new beauty, it will be the result of some fresh outpouring of spiritual force, such as occurred long ago in Egypt, later in Greece, in China following the introduction of Buddhism, and in Northern Europe during the two mystic centuries of the Middle Ages. Signs are not lacking that this change will come upon us too. The dense materiality of modern life is not necessarily an adverse factor; for of all paradoxes this is the most sublime, that good comes from evil, purity from corruption. The favorite food of epicures springs from the dunghill; the unspeakable saturnalia of Imperial Rome had issue in Christian saints and martyrs. Already may be noted presages of change. In the familiar warmed and lighted chamber of our everyday environment we sit snugly content, playing at what we call the game of life, when suddenly, just when we fancied we were safest, we are rapt out of ourselves into the infinite beatitude, as a fevered gambler might be summoned from his table by some beautiful, veiled woman, who leads him out into the cool, illimitable night.

After such an experience, life can never be the same. You who have dreamed are forced to follow your dream—to realize it if you are an artist. From that day you are bound by an obligation which others do not and need not share. You can no longer dissipate your time and such talents as you possess in assimilating the popular taste in order to reproduce it. This would be a prostitution far more ignoble than that of the man who has never been thus elected to the service of beauty. To him, the fleshpots of the world, the price of a virtue which was never his; to you, the eternal quest, wherever it may lead.

Do not conceive of beauty in any narrow way, as limited to mere aesthetics. Seek out the things that thrill you and be sure that there is beauty in them, for the test of beauty is the measure of the joy it brings. Beauty is mystery and enchantment, the thing with star-dust on it. Learn to recognize the brush of its invisible wing, not alone in art galleries and concert halls, but in a face in a crowd, a song at twilight, moonrise, sunset; in the din and glare of cities as well as in the silence of great spaces; in the train taking its flight to the seaboard as well as in the crow taking its flight to the rooky wood.

Knowing not when nor in what questionable shape beauty may reveal itself, it behooves you to cultivate so wide a catholicity of taste that no manifestation, however strange and disturbing, may pass untested through the alembic of your mind. You should constantly strive to realize what I have called the organic ideal in the work of your hands, not permitting your personal power of invention to atrophy by continual copying of the work of others, no matter how beautiful nor how sanctioned by time that work may be. Of everything you create you should ask: first, is it sincere and expressive; second, is it beautiful *to you?*

Doubtless failure will crown your efforts more often than success. A pioneer and a precursor in a movement which, when all is said, may never move, the best that you can hope for is to labor at the foundation of a Palace of Art which will be reared, if it is reared at all, by other hands. Your reward will be that should the tide turn, while you live and work, from the ordered ideal to the organic, some part of the mighty current will flow through you, instead of tossing you relentlessly aside.

Because the word "Gothic" has been taken as the type of the art which is organic and "Renaissance" as a type of that which is arranged, there is still danger of misunderstanding. Comprehend clearly that in speaking of organic architecture I do not refer solely to the art as practiced during the Middle Ages; in speaking of Renaissance architecture I use it only as indicative of a habit of mind which is timeless. If we except the architecture of edifices of the established religion in which the Gothic style is traditional, and therefore appropriate, nothing could be more absurd than the use by us of the mere externals of the mediaeval Gothic style. The forms of classic and Renaissance architecture are, of the two, on the whole more appropriate and amenable to modern needs and conditions; and if we are sticklers for precedent, they are better justified. The architecture of the future, whether arranged or organic, will probably resemble neither Gothic nor Renaissance. If it springs from deep within the soul, it will unfold new and unimagined beauties. If it is a product of the purely rational consciousness, it will consist of additions to, and modifications of, the architecture which we already have.

Because spirituality is the source of all beauty, arranged architecture proceeds from and succeeds organic. When the mystic spirit which produces organic architecture departs, the forms of its creating survive by reason of their beauty, but they are meaninglessly employed. All of the time-honored forms and arrangements of our so-called classic architecture were originally organic. Nothing could be more organic than the colonnade of a Grecian temple; nothing could be less so than the same colonnade with an iron stanchion buried in each column and the lintel held up by concealed steel beams.

Now, while it is necessary to draw these distinctions, and even to insist upon them, there is a higher synthesis in which they disappear. Every masterpiece disdains and defies classification. If it succeeds, we know that whatever the means and methods, they can be only the right ones and are their own sufficient justification. As a matter of fact, every architectural masterpiece, whatever its style or period, is both organic and arranged. However artificial it may be, it obeys some organic law of the mind; however naturalistic, it is full of self-conscious artifice.

In art there is a demonic element which places it above and beyond all man-made classifications and categories. The true artist is guided by an over-soul, whether he acknowledges or whether he denies its sway.

> The passive master lent his hand
> To the vast soul that o'er him planned.

It is this larger aspect of the whole subject which I propose to treat in my next lecture. In it I shall occupy myself, not with differences, but with identities. I shall attempt to discover the unchanging principles which determine every kind of formal beauty, to indicate the rudiments of the grammar of that language through which every thought of the human mind which writes itself on space must needs be expressed.

VI

THE LANGUAGE OF FORM

In my previous lecture I tried to make you acutely conscious of the confusion of tongues which attends the building of our towers of Babel, and I endeavored to arouse you to the need of developing a form-language which should be to the modern world what Greek architecture was to Pagan Greece, Gothic architecture to Christian Europe. As a preliminary to this high endeavor, let us seek to discover some of the unchanging principles which are at the root of every kind of beauty—in other words, to formulate the rhetoric of spatial expression.

The first and chief of these principles is undoubtedly that of unity; for the potency of any work of art is measured largely by the singleness of its appeal. An Egyptian pyramid, for example, has unity, but this quality is inherent in a Greek temple as well. In the case of the pyramid, the means whereby the effect of unity is produced are clear: every line leads to the summit; all converge into a single visible point. In the case of the Greek temple, the means remain a mystery to the beholder, but, as a matter of fact, in principle they are the same. The difference is that in the latter case the focal point is not visible; it is a point in space, high aloft in the air. Most of you probably know that the columns of the Parthenon all have a slight inclination inward. They are not parallel, but convergent; and if their axes were prolonged they would at last intersect. I do not claim, of course, that the effect of unity is solely due to this artifice; but this artifice is a contribution to it. As a symbol, it is magnificent. All manifoldness proceeds from and returns to the invisible where it is one.

This matter of invisible focal points is highly important. Did you ever think that somewhere in the air under the great open eye of the roof of the Roman Pantheon is a point which determined every arc of the curve of the giant dome; that somewhere in the ruined arena of the Colosseum are the two foci which determined the sweep of its circumscribing walls; that aloft in the apse of a Gothic cathedral is a point to which all its vaults converge and from which they seem to emanate? About the center of the central arch of most of the best triumphal arches is described a greater circle which determines the main proportions of the rectangular structure. These and similar artifices aid in co-ordinating the edifice into one memorable impression.

If unity is the first and controlling principle of a form-language, what is the second? Before we come to that, let us ask ourselves what a form-language is. It is some aggregation of symbols, borrowed from nature or fabricated by art, in endless variety of combination, for the expression of some ideal thing. By means of these symbols the inner spirit of life is drawn into a kind of diagrammatic representation of its nature and gets itself externalized—made flesh, so to speak. But behind the forms and arrangements employed, whether they are natural or artificial, are geometrical forms and arrangements; for "Nature geometrizes," as Emerson says. A form-language, therefore, may be reduced to geometry in the same way that a spoken language may be resolved into sounds and combinations of sounds. Just as sounds may be classified as vowel and consonant, so may forms be classified as straight (rectilinear) and curved, masses as light and dark, or as void and solid, producing the effect of light and dark. Colors, similarly, are warm and cold, brilliant and neutral, gay and grave.

This, then, is our second principle, duality—the polarity of related opposites. Before applying this principle to composition, let us discriminate between the different kinds of composition.

For our purposes, there are three kinds: line composition, mass composition—that is, *notan*, light and dark—and color composition. In a sense these correspond to line, plane, and solid—spaces of one, two, and three dimensions. Linear composition involves neither of the other two; *notan* composition, being concerned with light and dark masses, cannot dispense with line, for lines bound these masses; color composition combines both line and mass. As the method of the mind is to proceed from the simple to the complex, the Japanese, those masters of composition, in producing their designs devote themselves first to the problem of line rhythms, then to the disposition of their lights and darks; and finally to color harmony, though they keep all three things in mind simultaneously, as is necessary for a successful issue; otherwise these things interfere with and destroy one another.

Since I have mentioned Japanese art, let us take for our first illustration of the law of duality, or polarity, one of Hiroshige's best-known color prints, "The Pine Tree on an Island" (see Fig. 1). It is so faithful a rendering of the subject that a Japanese, seeing the print in my office, exclaimed, "I have been to that place, I have seen that wonderful old tree." And yet, though so true to nature, it is a piece of self-conscious art. The

PINE TREE ON AN ISLAND—HIROSHIGE

FIG. I

BAS-RELIEF OF ATHENA AND HER OWL

FIG. 2

line composition is as simple and uncompromising as could well be—the vertical lines of the straight-falling rain, the horizontal lines of the water, and the island, in strong contrast to the irregular curved outline of the pine tree. The mass composition is not less simple and conforms to, and accentuates, the line composition—the light sky, the darker water and embankment, the dark foliage. These three in color are, respectively, gray, blue, and black. With nothing to mitigate this cold color scheme, however, the law of polarity would not be honored by a due observance, so the artist has introduced a note of dull red in the upper left-hand corner—a matter of no pictorial significance, but necessary to the color harmony of the whole.

My second example, a bas-relief of Athena with her owl—Attic work of about 465 B.C. (see Fig. 2)—exhibits the same artful juxtaposition of straight lines and curves, even more simply disposed and contrasted. There is here the same regard for related masses, and, though unfortunately the color has disappeared (it was once colored; for the end of the spear was apparently painted on), we cannot doubt that the law of color contrast received recognition too.

It was the all but universal practice of artists of the great age of the Renaissance to display their figures in an architectural setting, for this was the most obvious and effective way of achieving the contrast between geometrical and flowing forms to which I call your attention. I need not show examples, for you yourselves will recall any number. Instead, I shall exhibit a photograph of a painting of later date, David's exquisite portrait of Madame Récamier, which, by reason of the obviousness of its composition, is related more nearly to the examples you have already seen (see Fig. 3). Note how the gracious curve of the womanly figure is enhanced by its contrast with the long horizontal line of the couch and by the vertical standard of the candelabrum.

Transferring our attention now to architecture, we find in this familiar combination of arch and engaged order the same polarity of which I speak (see Fig. 4). From these simple elements "has been expanded the architectural art, as a great and superb language wherewith man has expressed, through the generations, the changing drift of his thoughts." In the Romanesque portal of Saint Trophime at Arles you find those elements more beautifully, because more logically, arranged (see Fig. 5). Learn to give them instant recognition, wherever encountered, be it in such a grand combination as is exhibited by the cam-

PORTRAIT OF MADAME RÉCAMIER—J. LOUIS DAVID

FIG. 3

panile of St. Mark's against the long horizontal and many-domed church of St. Mark, or in so small a thing as a simple egg and dart. The source and secret of beauty are the same in both cases—contrasting straight and curved forms.

FIG. 4

The third law to which I would direct your attention is the law of trinity. It is latent, as you already doubtless discern, in polarity—for everything is from its very nature twofold; but while the semicircular arch changes imperceptibly from vertical to horizontal, and therefore may be considered a unit, vertical and horizontal lines cannot be thus reconciled and must be recognized as independent. Therefore we have in architecture three elements: lines vertical, horizontal, and curved.

Now there is a secret potency which appears to reside in the number three itself. At least three notes are necessary for full harmony in music, the three primary colors for complete color harmony, and the trinity of vertical, horizontal, and curved lines for architectural harmony. Three straight lines are the least number which will inclose a space. The geometrical correlative of the number three is naturally the triangle, and particularly the equilateral triangle. This figure, for which the eye has an especial fondness, is everywhere present in the arts of design, sometimes clearly displayed, more often obscurely. It performs the function of uniting and co-ordinating the various parts of a design in a manner analogous to that in which the accompaniment carries along and co-ordinates an air. So universal was the recognition of this need of the eye during the great age of Renaissance painting that the pyramidal composition became one of its conventions. Introduced by Fra Bartolomeo, it continued to be employed to and through the decadence. You all recall plenty of examples, but to show you just what I mean I call your attention to the triangular synopsis of Andrea del Sarto's "Madonna del Sacco" (see Fig. 6).

Architecture, of whatever style and period, is rich in similar examples. Out of many hundreds I show only one: the perfect little Erechtheum

DOORWAY, CHURCH OF SAINT TROPHIME, ARLES

FIG. 5

MADONNA DEL SACCO—ANDREA DEL SARTO

Fig. 6

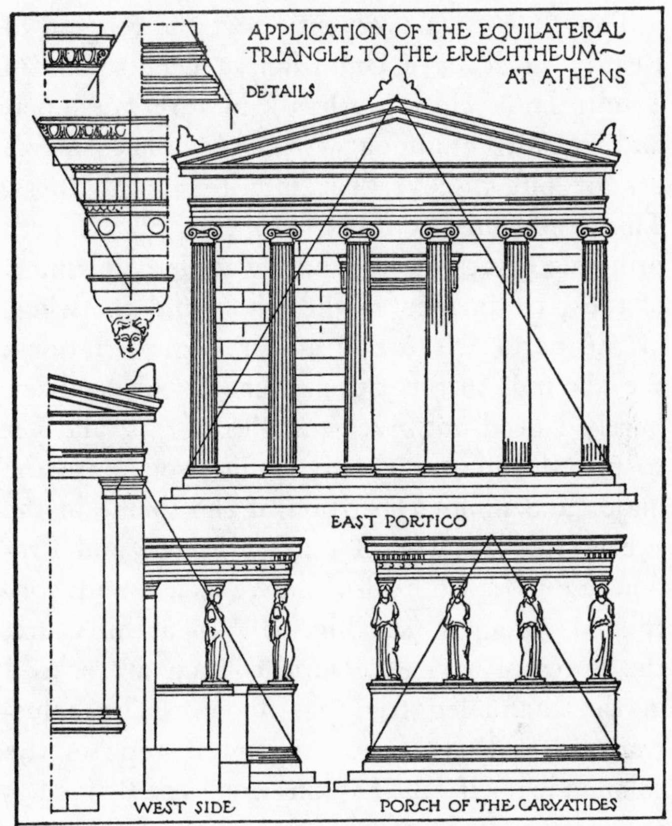

Fig. 7

of the Athenian Acropolis (see Fig. 7). The main proportions of French cathedrals were determined by this sort of triangulation, both in plan and in section, as Viollet le Duc has shown in the first volume of his *Discourses*.

Thus it is that every priest of the religion of Beauty must be a Unitarian, a Dualist, and a Trinitarian. He is no less a Nature-worshiper, and in his communion with her visible forms he cannot but discover her infinite manifoldness. This leads him to the perception of a fourth principle of aesthetics, that of variety in unity, of the part imaged in the whole and the whole in the part. Nature is an air with variations; she abounds in repetitions, echoes, consonances. Surely I need not give examples of this, and yet to put the matter clearly before you, note the major and minor repetition of the theme in the subsidiary details of Titian's "Sacred and Profane Love"; note also the reversed and contrasted triangles (see Fig. 8). In architecture, the flutes of a Greek Doric column are echoed in the channeled triglyphs above. The balustrade of a Renaissance colonnade repeats the colonnade itself; the flanking domes of Brunelleschi's great dome of the cathedral of Florence prepare the eye for the mighty upward sweep.

The fifth principle to which I would direct your attention is not less obvious and universal, but it is one for which it is difficult to find a name. Call it rhythmic diminution. This law is in the eye itself; for any series of equal and regular units, such as a row of columns and their

SACRED AND PROFANE LOVE—TITIAN

Fig. 8

intercolumniations, for example, when viewed in perspective become rhythmically unequal. They diminish as they recede from the eye, according to a mathematical law. This law is in the ear itself; for any musical note dies away into harmonics, each one fainter and higher than the last. Observe a column of smoke rising in still air. It puts forth spirals, these spirals split up into smaller spirals, and so on. A tree segregates, in the same way, into branches and the branches into twigs. These things will give you an idea of what I mean by rhythmic diminution. In architecture it is illustrated by the entasis of a column, by the diminishing spiral of an Ionic volute, by the artifice of superimposing the slenderer and more ornate orders on the simpler and sturdier. The most perfect and complete expression is found perhaps in a Gothic cathedral, which from a simple and massive substructure rears a veritable lacework of pinnacles against the sky. Gothic architecture and Gothic tracery rise flamelike, growing more intricate and wonderful as they ascend.

The sixth principle is that of radiation. Radiation is the arrangement of the units of a composition with reference to focal points—the relation of variables to some invariable. This, too, is in the eye itself and in the ear itself; for all horizontal lines in architecture appear to converge at the point of sight on the horizon, and in music the air returns to the tonic note of the scale. In radiation we return by a long detour to our starting-point, unity. They are opposite aspects of one and the same thing. You may say that all the lines of a pyramid lead from base to apex, but it is no less true that from the apex all lines lead to the base.

To illustrate the universality of these six principles in art, and to fix them more firmly in your mind by a recapitulation, I show you in what manner they are obeyed and illustrated in an acknowledged masterpiece of painting, Leonardo's "Last Supper" (see Fig. 9). It has *unity:* it poignantly portrays a dramatic moment in the life of the Savior of mankind. The various parts are fused by the creative fire in the soul of the artist into one memorable impression. *Duality* is achieved by the time-honored device of placing the figures in an architectural setting; the long horizontal of the table, the vertical panels of the walls, are what the accompaniment is to the air. *Trinity* appears in the three openings of the background, the arrangement of the twelve disciples in four groups of three figures each, and in the inclosure of the central figure of Christ in an equilateral triangle.

THE LAST SUPPER—LEONARDO DA VINCI

Fig. 9

By the law of *consonance* this triangle is echoed, as it were, in the triangular supports of the table and in the triangular synopses to which the groups of figures variously submit themselves. The great drama is broken up into a number of individual dramas, portrayed on the faces of the disciples as the Master utters the fateful words, "One of you shall betray me." *Rhythmic diminution* is illustrated in the diminishing lengths and sizes of the wall panels and the ceiling beams; and *radiation*, by reason of the fact that the point of sight of the whole composition, to which all the horizontal lines vanish, is in the figure of Christ.

I do not claim that every masterpiece illustrates these laws in this completeness and perfection, but no masterpiece was ever created which does not illustrate some of them. They need not have been present in the mind of the artist who conceives the work, nor of the observer who contemplates it, in order to exercise their potent magic. You should know about them because they constitute the mode and method whereby the spirit of life writes itself in materiality. I do not claim that they constitute the only mode and method. Other laws there are, no less fundamental and universal. Books have been written upon the spiral line in nature and art; numerical ratios, corresponding to the consonant musical intervals, properly constitute part of the rhetoric of the language of form; but these things I can only mention, for I must now pass to the consideration of the second necessary element in a language of form—ornament.

A complete and adequate form-language consists, first, in a system of construction expressing itself in appropriate forms, and a system of ornament, though it is true that these two things are sometimes so vitally related as to be scarcely separable. The architectural forms come of themselves—they are a matter of orderly evolution—but this is not so true of ornament. Ornament depends less upon structural necessity than upon psychology. It is the psychological mood objectively presented or expressed. This is the reason why any mutilated and time-worn fragment out of the great past, when art was a living language, can be assigned with certainty to its place and its period. The connoisseur has no difficulty in discriminating between Chinese, Hindu, Egyptian, Greek, and Etruscan ornament, because in each the soul of a people found adequate and appropriate utterance. The fact that today, when it comes to the question of ornament, we are content to adorn our creations with the grave-clothes of whatever dead style suits our fancy is simply one proof the more that we have no form-language of our own. While the development of architecture along new lines may safely be left to necessity and time and is already just beyond the horizon, the same is not true of ornament. We have done nothing in this field of any value whatever. We have not even tried to do anything, but have been perfectly content to beg the whole question. It is clear that we can do so no longer; but in what direction shall we seek?

Three alternatives suggest themselves: first, a new ornamental mode might be the creation of some wonderfully gifted individual; second, it could be derived from nature; third, it might be developed from geometry. Let us consider each of these alternatives. The first we must summarily reject. Even supposing the advent of a personal savior in this field, the imposition of the idiosyncratic space rhythm of a single individual upon an entire architecture would be unfortunate. Genius does not propagate itself; it descends neither from father to son nor from teacher to disciple. In Mr. Sullivan, for example, we have an ornamentalist of the highest originality and distinction, quite aside from his sterling qualities as an architect; but his secret is incommunicable, his disciples either imitate his mannerisms or they develop a manner and a method of their own. This leaves us with our problem unsolved. We do not want an ornament which is individual, but one which is universal; not one which has style, but one which *is* a style.

Consider now the second suggestion: shall we be able to find what we seek by conventionalizing natural forms? There is precedent for such a procedure. The Egyptian lotus, the Greek honeysuckle, the Indian palmette, the acanthus, achieved their apotheoses in art. Even today in Japan, where art is still a living language, the bamboo, the chrysanthemum, the wistaria, are successfully used as motifs for ornament. I think it would be a very good thing if the problem of the conventionalization of our native fruits and flowers were given to art students instead of the botanizing of old dry specimens. This has been done and is being done to some extent, but as a solution of the problem of ornament, it offers one difficulty which should not be overlooked. Today the native flora of a country loses much of its distinctive quality by reason of scientific agriculture and intensive cultivation under glass, coupled with ease and rapidity in the matter of transportation. Corn, buckwheat, tobacco, though indigenous to America, are less distinctively so than they once were. Moreover, our divorce from nature is more complete—so much so that dwellers in the city, where the giant flora of architecture for the most part raise their skyscraping heads, are more familiar with corn in the can than corn on the cob; they know buckwheat only in the form of buckwheat cakes; and not one smoker in ten would recognize tobacco as it grows in the fields. This vitiates, though it does not veto, recourse to natural forms for ornament.

The third alternative remains to be considered, and, to my thinking, it is that in which resides the richest promise. Let us consider it with care. Geometry has furnished, not one system of ornament, but many. A great deal of Chinese and Hindu ornament is rigidly geometrical; Moorish ornament is almost exclusively so. Gothic tracery is nothing but combinations of straight lines, circles, and the arcs of circles. The interesting development of decorative art which has taken place in Germany of late years makes use of little else but the square and the circle, the parallelogram and the ellipse. These systems, all derived from geometry, are widely different from one another. What has been done can be done; geometry may provide us with

PATTERN DERIVED FROM GROUPED CUBES

FIG. 10

the very thing we seek. The problem is simply one of selection and development. How shall we set about our task? For we are in the position of Sinbad in the valley of diamonds; we are surrounded by treasure of which we do not know how to possess ourselves.

Ornament must not only satisfy the aesthetic sense, but it must be symbolically significant. This can be accomplished if in some way ornament can be made to indicate the trend of consciousness—if some relation can be established between ornament and psychology. This may seem at first thought an impossible proposition, but perhaps it is not so impossible as it appears. Do not think that I am only juggling with words when I suggest that the problem may be solved by recourse to the fourth dimension of space.

A BAY WINDOW

FIG. 11

THE LANGUAGE OF FORM

This is a phrase of varied and ambiguous meanings, often heard, yet little understood—understood least, perhaps, by those who use it most. To the mathematician it means a direction at right angles to every one of the so-called three dimensions of space. By the man on the street it is used to describe anything which is arcane and mysterious.

But behind this loose use of a loose phrase lies a true intuition: the intuition, namely, that the modern mind, so lately exclusively scientific, enamored of mere facts, has taken a turn in a new direction at right angles to every direction known heretofore. The past few years have witnessed the rebirth of wonder. Science, scornful of the occult, has now an occult of its own to deal with. Philosophy, hopeless of translating life through the reason in terms of inertia, perceived a universal flux, the meaning of which the intuition alone can grasp; and religion, abandoning its narrow orthodoxies and man-made moralities of a superior prudence, seeks the mystical experience above and before all. To each the best thing in the world has come to seem something out of it. Our House of Life, where we had thought to dwell always more snug and content, is haunted by footfalls from another world. Now the fourth dimension of

PATTERN DERIVED FROM THE 600-HEDROID

FIG. 12

the mathematician is a perfect symbol of this land which is "back of the north wind and behind the looking glass." The sublime idea that the personal self of each one of us is but the transitory manifestation on the plane of materiality of an immortal individual whose habitat is on higher planes of being, has its analogue in the mathematical conception that all three-dimensional figures are projections on three-dimensional space of four-dimensional forms. That is, the sphere is the projection of the hyper-sphere, the cube of the hyper-cube, and so on, in the same way that the circle may be considered

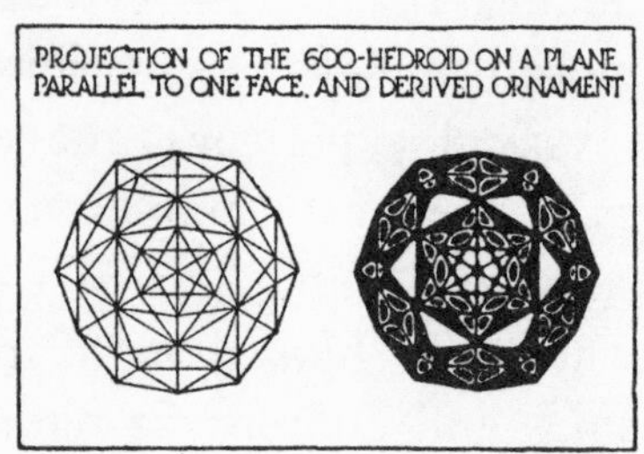

PROJECTION OF THE 600-HEDROID ON A PLANE PARALLEL TO ONE FACE, AND DERIVED ORNAMENT

FIG. 13

AN ORGAN CASE

Fig. 14

as the plane projection of the sphere, the square of the cube. The elements of four-dimensional figures are known to mathematics. Their projection in spaces of lower dimensions is a matter of no great difficulty. What I propose, therefore, is to derive from these projections material for ornament, and in so doing to symbolize the dominant fact of the modern world, that we are attempting to explore that reality from which we are shut off by the limitations of our sensuous mechanism.

Four-dimensional geometry is as real a thing and richer far than three-dimensional geometry, bearing the same relation to the latter as that does to plane geometry. It is indeed so rich a field that only a few of the most elementary figures and configurations are sufficient to furnish the ornamentalist with all the material he needs.

To explain these figures in detail and the method of their representation would be impossible within the limits of this lecture. To make them fully intelligible would require more time than is at my disposal and the assistance of numerous models and diagrams. I can show you only a few of the achieved results (see Figs. 10–16). This failure to gratify your curiosity as regards method is unimportant; for with patience and intelligence you can develop a method of your own, in case the examples I show you have the good fortune to please your aesthetic sense. That is the final test, and if you fail to find here the needed element of beauty my labor has been in vain, my logic false, and my philosophy futile. If, however, you find here hints and intimations of a beauty which does not submit itself to classification in any of the familiar categories to which labels have already been attached, I commend the whole matter to your attention as a possible contribution to the form-language of the future. It possesses the following advantages: first, the one already dwelt upon—the relation of the ornamental mode to the psychological mood; second, the richness of the field, of

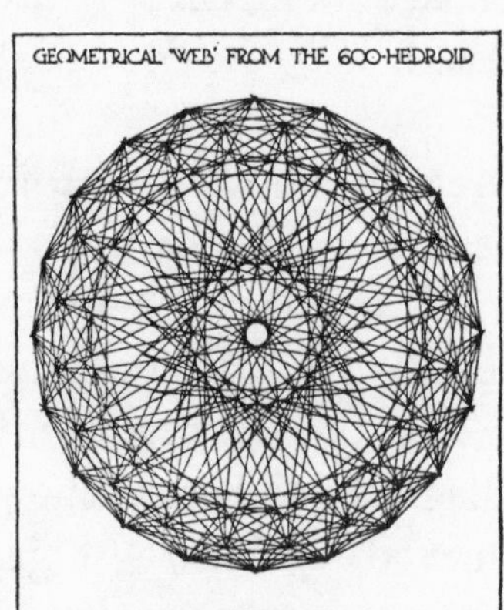

FIG. 15

THE WATER GATE

Fig. 16

which you may gain some idea by comparing solid geometry with plane geometry, four-dimensional geometry being related to solid geometry in a manner analogous to this; third, the opportunities offered for originality and the expression of individuality within wise and reasonable limits. The principle once assimilated, every designer would inevitably apply it in an individual manner, and yet just by reason of its being founded upon a principle and not a whim, there would result that family resemblance which we always discern in the work of individuals working within the limits of what we name a style; fourth, the principles and method are communicable, teachable, and though without the aid of a highly developed aesthetic sense no fine result is possible, it gives to that sense the material and a method.

GROUP:
TETRAHEDRONS AND DERIVED ORNAMENT
FIG. 17

There is another source of ornament which I may mention, of not less symbolical value, for

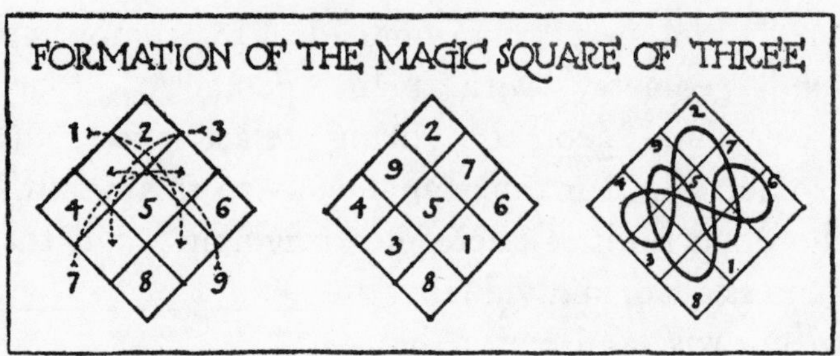

Fig. 18

it has occult associations. I refer to magic lines in magic squares. You all know what a magic square is: it is a sort of numerical acrostic, an arrangement in square form of numbers which yield the same magic sum when added in vertical and horizontal columns and along the diagonals. Magic squares are of very ancient origin. There is one carved in stone on an old temple gate in India. Albrecht Dürer introduced one into his engraving of "Melancholia," and they are known to have occupied the minds of mediaeval philosophers and mystics. Today one finds them in the puzzle departments of the magazines, and the principle of their formation has engaged the attention of the followers of pure

Fig. 19

mathematics. Now every magic square contains a magic line, found by following the numbers in their natural order from square to square. These magic lines are often very interesting and even beautiful, exhibiting an intricate and unusual type

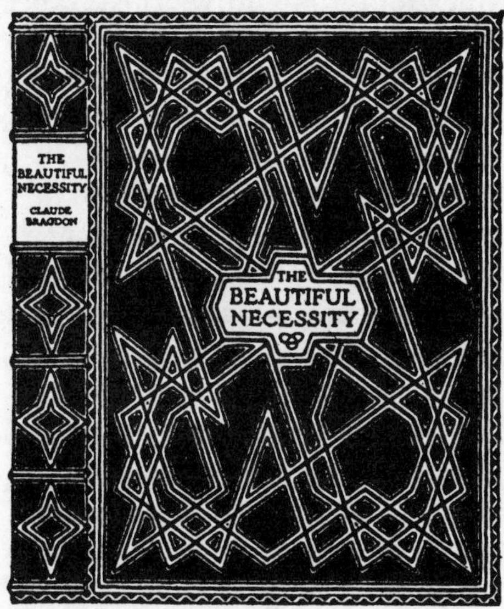

BOOK COVER DESIGN BASED ON THE KNIGHT'S TOUR OR MAGIC SQUARE OF EIGHT

FIG. 20

of symmetry. Translated into curves and interlaced, they are so strongly reminiscent of Celtic interlaces that it suggests the possibility that Celtic ornament may have been developed according to this method. Another curious fact in this connection is that Dürer, who, as we know, was interested in magic squares, devoted some of his inexhaustible industry to the designing of interlacing knots.

The decorative value of many magic lines is beyond question. To prove this, I need show you only one or two: the first and simplest, that derived from the magic square of three; the second, a magic square of four (see Fig. 19), and a decorative treatment of the line traced by the knight in making what is known as the knight's tour on the chessboard (see Fig. 20). This is a familiar feat of chess-players. It consists in starting at any square, and by the knight's move (two squares forward and one to right or left) touching at each square once and returning to the starting-point. This path or track is really a magic line of a magic square, and the trick is done by remembering sixty-four numbers in a certain order. Kellar, the magician, used to introduce this trick in his performances.

Now as the number of magic squares is practically limitless, and as each of them yields a magic line, you can readily see that there is much matter for the designer of ornament, even though all magic lines do not lend themselves to his particular purpose.

Besides appropriate and beautiful structural forms, appropriate and beautiful ornament, a form-language should possess a third element, that of color. The great ages of great art reveled in color, and each developed it in a distinctive way. A Roman bath, a Greek temple, the interior of a Gothic cathedral, were gorgeous with color. Today, in our architecture, we beg the whole question of color. It is a confession of our incompetence—we are afraid. Into this question of color I cannot go in a constructive way. To do so, even if I could, does not fall within the limits—already overpassed—which I have assigned to this lecture. I simply note the necessity and leave it there.

These matters to which I have called your attention are after all only bright pebbles picked up almost at random on the shoreless ocean of beauty, whose tides forever flow beneath the very casements of our House of Life. Our aesthetic poverty is of our own making; we can end it at any moment by utilizing the beauty everywhere at hand. There is nothing more absurd than to suppose that our age is bankrupt of beauty. It is pre-eminently an age of power, and power at the ordained season translates itself to beauty in men's souls and thence flows into visible and ponderable forms. "There is a fount about to stream." Out of modern civilization, chastened by suffering and sacrifice, awed into reverence by supernal revelations, stirred into hope by an immanent divine, man will weave new patterns on the loom of space just as he did anciently in China, in Assyria, in Egypt, and in Greece.

This is the artist's work, and let every artist in this audience rededicate himself to the task. As was said by Emerson, our great high priest, of that beauty which endures, "Fear not the new generalization."